CHILDREN'S DICTIONARY

This edition published 1983 by
Book Club Associates
By arrangement with Granada Publishing Limited

Copyright © Ronald Ridout
Illustrations copyright © Granada

Printed in Italy by
New Interlitho, Milan

Ronald Ridout's
CHILDREN'S
DICTIONARY

Book Club Associates
London

abcdefghijk
xyz ABCDE
NOPQRST

mnopqrstuvv

FGHIJKLM

UVWXYZ a

Aa

aardvark a South African mammal

abandon 1. to give up
2. to leave and not return to

abbey 1. a place where monks or nuns live
2. a church

monk

abbreviation the short form of a word (Mrs, St., Fri., P.T.O. and a.m. are all abbreviations.)

able 1. having the power (He wasn't able to lift the rock as it was too heavy.)
2. clever (He is a very able mechanic.)
ably, ability, abilities

aboard on a ship, a train or an aircraft

abolish to do away with

aborigine one of the first inhabitants of a country, especially of Australia

about 1. roughly (It happened about a week ago.)
2. to do with (I told him all about the film.)

above over; higher than

abreast one beside the other

abroad in another country

absent away; not here
absence, absent-minded, absentee

absolutely completely

absurd silly, clearly not true

abundant plentiful; in great quantity
abundance, abundantly

accent 1. emphasis
2. the tone in which people speak

accept to take what is offered you
acceptable, acceptance

accident something unpleasant that is not expected
accidental, accidentally

accompany to go with (His photo accompanied the letter.)
accompaniment, accompanies, accompanied

accomplish to complete a task successfully
accomplished, accomplishment

according to judging from what someone says (According to Vicky, this is where John lives.)

accordion a musical instrument with a keyboard and airbag

account 1. a description (Bob gave an account of what he did.)
2. a paper showing money you owe; a bill

accurate exact; correct in every way
accuracy, accurately

accuse to say someone has done wrong (She accused me of breaking her crayon.)

accused, accusing, accuser,
accusation
ace 1. the highest playing card
2. a person who is very good at
something
ache 1. a lasting pain
2. to have a pain like this
ached, aching, head-ache,
tooth-ache
acid 1. very sharp in taste
2. a substance that tastes sour and
can burn
acorn the nut of an oak tree
acre a surface measurement that is a
little smaller than a football pitch
acquaintance a person you know
slightly
acrobat a person who does clever
balancing tricks in a circus or on the
stage
across 1. from one side to the other
(We walked across the new bridge.)
2. on the other side of (The shop is
just across the road.)
act 1. to take a part in a play
2. to do something (We must act
quickly if we want to find the lost
puppy.)
3. a deed; something done
action something that somebody does
(His action in taking the money was
very wrong.)
active showing action; busy
activity, activities, actively
actor a man who takes part in a play
actress a woman who takes part in a
play
actual real (It looked solid, but in actual
fact it was quite hollow.)
actually, actuality
acute sharp (Dogs have an acute sense
of smell.)
acutely, acuteness
add to count up; to join on
addition, additionally

adder a poisonous snake
address details of where someone lives
addresses
adequate enough for the purpose
adhere to stick to
adhesive 1. sticking fast
2. a sticky substance; a glue
adjective a word that describes a noun
(A *tall* building.)
adjectival, adjectivally
admiral the highest-ranking officer in
the navy
admire to think highly of (We admired
him for speaking out against
wrong.)
admiration, admirably, admiring,
admirable
admit 1. to allow to enter
2. to agree (I admit I was wrong.)
admittance, admitted, admittedly,
admission, admitting
adopt 1. to take on an idea
2. to take on a child as one's own
adore to love very much
adorable, adorably, adoration,
adoring
adrift drifting helplessly
adult 1. a grown-up person
2. grown up
advance to go foward
advancement, advanced, advancing
advantage anything making for success
(It is an advantage to speak a
foreign language.)
advantageous
adventure an exciting happening
adventurous, adventurer,
adventuresome

adverb a word that tells us about the action of a verb (She danced *beautifully.)*

advertise to make well known *advertisement, advertising*

advice what we suggest people should do (My advice is to go and see a doctor.)

advise to make suggestions to help (She advised me to see a doctor.) *advisable, advising, advised*

aerial a wire frame to pick up or send radio or television signals

aerodrome an old-fashioned name for an airfield with buildings; a small airport

aeroplane an aircraft (It is often called an airplane in the USA)

affection love or great liking

afford to have enough money to buy something (We can't afford a new car yet.)

afloat 1. floating
2. on a moving ship

afraid frightened

aged, aging (or *ageing), ageless*

aggravate 1. to make worse
2. to annoy
aggravated, aggravating, aggravation

ago in the past (It happened long ago.)

agree 1. to think the same as someone
2. to say yes (We agreed to help him.)
agreeable, agreeably, agreeing, agreement

agriculture farming
agricultural

ahead in front of

aid 1. help
2. to give help

aim 1. to get ready to hit something
2. the thing you try to do (My aim is to become a pilot.)
aimless, aimlessly

air 1. what we breathe
2. to make sure clothes are dry
3. a tune
airborne, airless, air-tight, airy, airily

after 1. at a later time
2. behind
afternoon, afterwards, afterthought

again once more

against 1. opposite to
2. beside

age 1. how old you are
2. a special period of time in history (The Bronze Age)

aircraft a flying machine; an aeroplane
aircrew, airfield, airline, airmail, airport, airship, airworthy, airworthiness

ajar partly open

alarm 1. to frighten
2. the feeling of fear
3. a warning signal, such as a fire alarm

album 1. a book to hold stamps, photos, etc
2. a record with several songs or tunes

alert watchful, ready to act

alight 1. on fire
2. to step down from a train, bus, etc.

alike looking the same

alive living, lively

all the whole, everyone, everything

alley a narrow road between houses

alligator an American reptile like a crocodile

allotment a small piece of land for growing vegetables

allow to let someone do something
allowable, allowance

ally a friend or country supporting you
allies

almost nearly

alone all by yourself

along from one end to the other
alongside

aloud not silent, so that people can hear

alphabet all the letters of a language
alphabetical, alphabetically

already by this time

also too; as well

altar a holy table in a place of worship where offerings are made to God

alter to change
alterable, alteration

although though; in spite of

altogether 1. completely (He was altogether wrong about the berries being poisonous.)
2. counting everyone or everything (I have five uncles altogether.)

always at all times

amateur a person who does something for love and not for money

amaze to surprise very much
amazed, amazement, amazing

ambulance a large van or car to take sick or injured people to hospital

amen a word meaning 'so be it' at the end of a hymn or prayer

among, amongst 1. in the middle of
2. between (Divide them among you.)

amount 1. a number or quantity
2. the total

ample plenty for the purpose
amply

amuse to keep someone happy
amusement, amusing, amusingly

ancestor someone from whom you are descended
ancestral, ancestry

anchor a heavy hook dropped to stop a ship from drifting
anchorage

ancient very old; from times long ago

angel 1. a messenger from God
2. any very nice person
angelic, angelically

angry in a bad temper; very cross
anger, angrier, angriest, angriness

angle a corner where two lines meet

angler a fisherman using a rod and line

animal any living creature that is able to move by itself

ankle the joint between the leg and foot

anniversary the day of the year when you have a birthday or remember some other special occasion

announce to make something known
  publicly
    announcement, announcer,
    announcing
annoy to make someone cross
    annoyance
annual 1. happening every year
    2. a book that comes out once a year
    3. a plant that lives for only one year
another 1. one more
    2. a different one
answer 1. a reply or to reply
    2. the solution to a sum or problem
ant a small insect

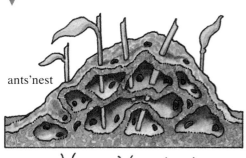

ants'nest

queen ant
worker ant
soldier ant

antelope an African mammal with
  horns
anti against
    anti-aircraft, anti-social, anticyclone
anxious 1. worried about what may
  happen
    2. wishing strongly (Tom was
    anxious to gain a place in the team.)
    anxiety, anxiously
any 1. some (Have you any money?)
    2. whichever you like (You can
    choose any book on this shelf.)
    anybody, anyhow, anyone,
    anything, anywhere
apart away from each other
apartment a flat, especially in the USA

gibbon

orang-utan

gorilla

chimpanzee

ape an animal like a large monkey with
  no tail
apologize to say you are sorry
apparatus machines or equipment
  used for a special purpose
apparent obvious
appeal 1. to beg for
    2. to be attractive (The idea
    appealed to us all.)
appear 1. to come into sight
    2. to seem to be (It appears to be
    alive.)
    appearance, apparent
appetite a desire for something,
  usually food
    appetizing
apple a kind of fruit
apply 1. to ask for (He applied for the
  job.)
    2. to be connected with (Those rules

11

do not apply to this game.)
applies, applied, application,
applicant, applicable, appliance

appoint to choose someone for a job
appointment

approach to come near to
approaches, approachable

approve to be pleased with something
approval, approving

apricot a fruit like a peach

April the fourth month of the year

apron a piece of cloth worn in front of
the body to keep clothes clean

aquarium 1. a tank where live fish are
kept
2. a building where such tanks are
on show

arch the curved top of a bridge, door,
etc. *archway*

archer someone who uses a bow and
arrows

architect someone who designs
buildings

area the size of a flat space

argue to disagree in words
arguing, arguable, argument,
argumentative

arise to get up, to happen
arising, arisen, arose

arithmetic work done with numbers
arithmetical, arithmetically

arm 1. the part of the body between
the shoulder and the hand
2. *arms* is another word for weapons
armchair, armpit, armful, armless

armour a metal suit for protection in
war

army many soldiers fighting as one
group

arrange 1. to put things in order
2. to make plans (We arranged to
play football after school.)
arrangement, arranging,
arrangeable

arrest to take someone prisoner

arrive to reach the place you are going
to
arrival, arriving

arrow 1. a pointed stick shot from a
bow
2. a pointer in the shape of an arrow

art the ability to do such things as
paint, draw, sew
artistic

article 1. a thing on its own; an object
2. a piece written in a newspaper

artificial made by people; not natural
artificially, artificiality

artist a person who paints, draws,
plays music
artistic, artistically

ash 1. the powder left after burning
   2. a tall tree with grey bark
ashamed very sorry about something
ashore on the shore; on land
ask to call for an answer
asleep sleeping; not awake
aspirin medicine to lessen pain
ass a donkey
assault to attack suddenly
assemble to gather together
   assembly, assembling
assist to help
   assistance, assistant
astern at the back end of a ship
astonish to surprise greatly
astronaut a space-traveller

ate past tense of 'to eat'
atlas a book containing maps
   atlases
atmosphere the air around the Earth
atom a tiny piece of matter
   atomic
attach to fasten to
   attaches, attachment
attack to try to defeat; to set upon
attempt to try
attend 1. to be present

2. to listen to carefully
   attendance, attendant, attention,
   attentive
attic a room just under the roof
attitude the way you feel about something
attract 1. to get someone's attention
   2. to make things come closer
   (Magnets attract metal things.)
   attractive, attraction, attractively
audience the people who attend a play,
   concert, film, etc.
August the eighth month of the year
aunt your father or mother's sister, or
   your uncle's wife
   aunty, auntie
author the writer of a book
   authorship
authority 1. the power to give orders
   2. an expert (He is an authority on
   jewels.)
autograph a person's signature
autumn the season between summer
   and winter
   autumnal
avalanche a sudden fall of snow down
   a mountain
avenue a road with trees on both sides
average middle (The average score
   was 23.)
avoid to keep out of the way of
await to wait for
awake not asleep
   awaken
award a prize
aware knowing about something (He
   was not aware that he had trodden
   on my toe.)
awful very bad; terrible
   awfully, awfulness
awkward clumsy; not moving well
   awkwardly, awkwardness
axe a tool for chopping wood
   axing, axman
axle the rod on which wheels turn

Bb

baby a very young child
  babe, babies, babyish, babyishness
baby-sitter a person who looks after young children when their parents are out
bachelor an unmarried man
back 1. the rear part; not the front
  2. the part of the body between the shoulders and the bottom
  3. a defending player in football
  4. in return (He gave me back my pen.)
  5. to go backwards; to reverse
  backbone, backfire, backside, backstroke,
backward making less than normal progress
backwards in a reverse direction
bacon smoked meat from the back or sides of a pig
badge a sign worn to show you belong to a school or a club
badger 1. a burrowing animal
  2. to bother someone

badminton a game played with rackets and a shuttlecock
bag a container made of flexible material
  bagged, bagging, hand-bag, shopping-bag
baggage luggage
bagpipes a musical instrument with a windbag

bait food put on a hook to catch fish
bake to cook in an oven
  baker, baking, bakery
balance 1. to make something steady (The seal balanced a ball on its nose.)
  2. to remain steady (I balanced on one leg.)
  balancing, balancer
bale 1. a large bundle
  2. to scoop out water
ball 1. a round object for playing games
  2. a large party with dancing
ballet dancing that tells a story
balloon 1. a large ball filled with hot air or gas for lighter-than-air flight
  2. a small toy looking like this
ballot a vote taken using pieces of paper

bamboo tall stiff grass with hollow stems

banana a fruit with yellow skin (See page 59)

band 1. a strip of something, such as a rubber band
2. a stripe (band of colour)
3. a group of musicians
bandsman, bandstand, jazz band

bandage strip of material to bind a wound
bandaging, bandaged

bandit a robber who steals from travellers

bang 1. a heavy blow
2. a loud noise

bangle a bracelet

banjo a musical instrument (See page 90)

bank 1. the side of a river or pond
2. raised or sloping ground
3. a place that looks after people's money

banner a flag carried in a procession

banquet a large feast

baobab an African tree with a huge trunk (See page 144)

baptise to christen by dipping in water
baptised, baptising, baptism

bar 1. a long piece of something hard
2. a division in music
3. to block the way
4. a counter where drinks are sold
barred, barring, barman, barmaid

barbecue an open air party where food is cooked on a metal frame over a fire

barber a men's hairdresser

bare 1. not covered
2. just (a bare chance)
barely, bareness

bargain 1. an agreement to buy or sell
2. something bought unusually cheaply

barge a flat bottomed boat

bark 1. the cry of a dog
2. the covering of the trunk of a tree

barley a cereal (See page 29)

barn a building for storing things on a farm

barracks a place where soldiers live

barrel 1. a container with curved sides and flat ends
2. the metal tube of a gun
barrelful, barrel-shaped, barrelled

barren not producing anything (barren ground)

barrier a fence to stop people passing

barrow a small cart pushed by hand
barrowful, barrow-boy, wheelbarrow

base 1. the bottom of something
2. headquarters

baseball an outdoor game played mainly in the USA

basement a room below ground level

bashful shy
bashfully, bashfulness

basin a deep bowl for liquids

basket a container for carrying by hand
basketful, basket-ball, basket-work

bat 1. a piece of wood to hit a ball
  2. a night animal with wings
  batted, batting, batsman, batty
bath a container to sit in to wash
  bathroom, bath-tub, swimming-bath
bathe 1. to go swimming
  2. to wash gently (He bathed his sore thumb in warm water.)
  bather, bathing-costume, sunbathe
battery 1. something for storing electricity
  2. several guns used together
battle a fight between two armies
  battlefield, battleship, battle-axe
bay a curved part of the sea-shore
bazaar 1. a sale to raise money for charity
  2. a market in Eastern countries
beach the sand or pebbles at the edge of the sea or a lake

bead a small round object to make a necklace
beak the hard pointed part of a bird's mouth

beaker a tall glass or cup with no handle
beam a long thick bar of wood or metal
bean a pod vegetable (See page 151)
  bean bag, bean-feast, beanstalk
bear 1. a large wild animal
  2. to carry
  3. to put up with (I can't bear to be late.)
  4. to give birth
  bore, born, bearable, unbearable

polar bear

beard the hair growing on a man's face
bearded, beardless
beast 1. any four-footed animal
2. a cruel or badly behaved person
beastly, beastliness
beat 1. to hit again and again
2. to whip a mixture before cooking
3. a regular rhythm (You must
dance to the beat of the music.)
4. to defeat
beaten, beater, dead-beat,
beautiful very lovely or attractive
beautifully, beauty, beautify
beaver a furry water animal that makes

a river home called a lodge
because for the reason that
beckon to signal to someone to come
become come to be (It became very
dark.)
bed 1. something to sleep on
2. a piece of ground where plants are
grown
3. the bottom of the sea or a river
bedded, bedding, bedroom,
bed-ridden, bedside, bedstead,
bedtime, bed-clothes
bedouin people of a wandering desert
tribe

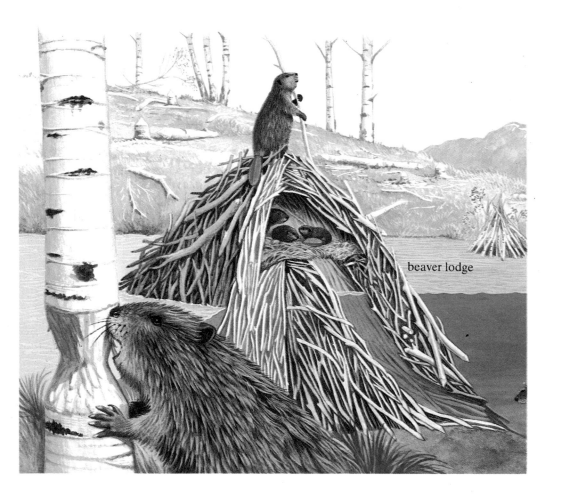

beaver lodge

bee

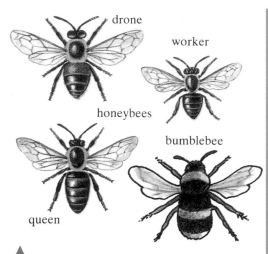

drone

worker

honeybees

bumblebee

queen

bee an insect that makes honey
beehive, beekeeper, beeswax
beech a tree (See page 145)
beef the meat from a cow or bull
*beefburger, beefsteak, beefy,
beefeater*
beer a drink made from barley, malt
and hops
beetroot a red root vegetable
beetle an insect with hard wings

before 1. earlier than
2. in front of
beg to ask for
beggar, begged, begging
begin to start
began, beginner, beginning, begun
behave 1. to act; to do (He is behaving
very oddly.)
2. to conduct oneself well (His
mother told him to behave himself or
leave the room.)
behaving, behaviour
behind 1. at the back of (He hid behind
the door.)
2. late (Mrs Lee was behind with her
work.)
believe to think that something is true
belief, believing, believer, believable
bell a hollow metal object that rings
when it is struck
bellow to roar like a bull
belong 1. to be owned by someone
(The camera belongs to me.)
2. to be in the proper place (The
milk belongs in the fridge.)
below underneath; lower than

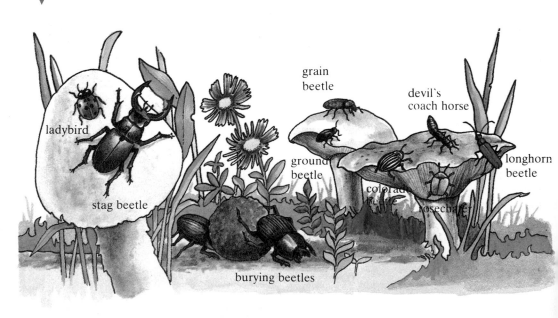

ladybird

stag beetle

burying beetles

grain
beetle

ground
beetle

colorado
beetle

devil's
coach horse

longhorn
beetle

rosechafer

18

belt a strip of material worn round the waist

bench 1. a long hard seat
2. a work table
benches

bend 1. to make something into a curved shape
2. to bow or stoop

beneath under; below

benefit to help or receive help (How will you benefit from this arrangement?)

berry a small fruit with seeds but no stone
berries, blackberry

berth a bed on a ship or train

beside at the side of; next to

besides as well as (I have another kite besides this one.)

best none better

bet to risk winning or losing money on the result of an event
betted, betting

betray to give someone up to the enemy

better more good (Tom's aim is better than mine.)

between in the middle of two things

beware to be careful of (Beware of the dog!)

beyond on the far side

Bible the holy book of Christians

bicycle a two-wheeled riding machine
bicycling, bicycled, bicyclist, bike

bill 1. a paper showing how much money is owed
2. a bird's beak

bind to tie up or wrap round

bingo a game of lucky numbers

birch a tree (See page 145)

bird an animal with wings and feathers (See pictures on pages 20, 21)

birth the act of being born
birthday, birth-mark, birth-place

biscuit a flat thin crisp cake

bishop a clergyman in charge of a large area

bison a kind of wild ox called a buffalo in the USA

bit 1. a small piece
2. the metal rod put into a horse's mouth

bite to cut with the teeth
biting, bitten

black the darkest colour
blackboard, blacken, blackmail, black-out

blade 1. the sharp part of a knife or tool
2. anything blade-shaped (a blade of grass)

blank not written on; plain

blanket a warm woolly bed-covering

blast 1. a sudden rush of air or sound
2. to blow up something with explosives
blast-off

blaze to burn brightly
blazing

blazer a kind of jacket

bleat to make a cry like a sheep or goat

bleed to lose blood

bless to wish someone happiness

blew past tense of 'to blow'

blind not able to see
blindfold, blindly, blindness

blink to close and open the eyes quickly

blister a bubbly swelling on the skin

canary

crow

dove

heron

jackdaw

kookaburra

magpie

nightingale

ostrich

swan

sparrow

starling

eagle

lark

rook

swift

thrush

blizzard a snowstorm with violent wind

blob a small drop or lump

block 1. a big piece (a block of wood) 2. a row of buildings (a block of flats) 3. to be in the way of something

blond, blonde a person with fair hair

blood the red liquid flowing through veins
bloodhound, bloodless, bloodshed, bloody, blood-stained, bloodshot, blood-thirsty

bloom to flower

blossom a mass of flowers on fruit trees

blot a spot of ink or other dirty mark
blotted, blotter, blotting

blouse a garment worn on the top part of the body, usually by girls and women

blow 1. to send air out of the mouth 2. to move air (The wind is blowing.) 3. a hit or hard knock (a blow on the head.)

blue a colour (The sky is blue.)
bluebell, bluebottle

blunder a silly or careless mistake

blunt not sharp

blush to go red in the face
blushes, blushing

board 1. a long flat piece of wood 2. to get on a boat, train or plane

boast to praise yourself too much
boastful, boastfully, boastfulness

boat a small ship
boatful, rowing-boat, fishing-boat, boat-hook, boatman, boat-race

bob to move up and down as if floating
bobbed, bobbing

body the whole of a person or animal
bodies, bodily, body-guard

bog wet and spongy ground
bogged, boggy

boil 1. to heat water till it bubbles

2. a painful swelling on the skin
boiled, boiler

bold 1. fearless
2. clearly seen
boldly, boldness

bolt 1. a fastening for a door
2. a thick pin on which a nut is threaded
3. to run away suddenly (The horse bolted.)

bomb a weapon that explodes
bomb-shell, bombard, bomber

bone one of the parts of a skeleton
bony, bone-dry, boneless

bonfire an outdoor fire for burning rubbish

bonnet 1. a kind of hat
2. the lid of a car's engine (hood in USA)

bonny looking healthy

book pages fastened inside a cover
bookcase, booklet, book-token

boomerang a curved wooden weapon that can return to the thrower

boot 1. a shoe that covers part of the leg
2. the luggage space in a car (trunk in USA)

border 1. an edge (the border of a skirt)
2. the line on a map between two countries
3. a narrow flower bed

bore 1. to make a hole (He bored with a drill.)
2. to make someone tired because you are not interesting
boredom, boring

born given life (The baby was born yesterday.)

borne from 'to bear' (She has borne a great burden, having an invalid husband.)

borrow to take something you know has to be given back

boss the chief or person in charge
bossy, bosses

both the one and the other

bother 1. to cause trouble (Don't bother me.)
2. to take trouble (She doesn't bother with her appearance.)

bottle a narrow-necked container for liquids
bottling, bottle-neck

bottom 1. the lowest part of anything
2. the part of the body you sit on
bottomless, bottom-most, rock-bottom

bough a branch of a tree

bought the past tense of 'to buy'

bounce to jump back when thrown against something
bounced, bounces, bouncing, bouncy

bound 1. to be certain (It is bound to be wet tomorrow.)
2. to leap (The kangaroo bounded away.)

boundary a line marking the edge of something (There is a fence on the boundary of his land.)
boundaries

bouquet a bunch of flowers

bow (rhyming with 'now') 1. to bend politely
2. the front part of a ship

bow (rhyming with 'go') 1. a knot made with loops (She tied the ribbon in a bow.)
2. a weapon that shoots arrows
3. a rod to play a violin

bowl 1. a dish or basin
2. to send the ball to the batsman

bow-legged having legs curved out at the knees

box 1. a container with straight sides
2. to fight with gloves
boxes, boxer, Boxing Day, box-office

boy a male child
boy-friend, boyhood, boyish
bracelet a decoration worn around the wrist
brag to boast
bragged, bragging, bragger, braggart
brain the matter in our heads with which we think
brainy, brain-wave, brainless
brake the part of a vehicle that makes it slow down or stop
braking
bramble a blackberry bush
branch a part of a tree that grows from the trunk; a bough
branches
brand 1. to make a mark with a red-hot iron
2. a particular make of goods
brass a yellow metal made by mixing copper and other metals
brassy, brass band
brave without fear
bravely, bravery
bray to make a noise like a donkey
bread food made by baking flour, yeast and water
bread-crumbs, breadwinner
break 1. to smash; to pull apart
2. a rest; an interval
breakable, breakage, breakdown, breaker, breakneck, breakwater
breakfast the first meal of the day
breath the air that is taken into the lungs
breathless, breathlessly
breathe to take air into the body and let it out again
breather, breathing
breed 1. to keep animals to produce young (Mrs Ash breeds pigs and sells the piglets.)
2. a kind of animal
bred, breeding, breeder

breeze a gentle wind
breezes, breezy
brick a block of baked clay for building
bride a woman on her wedding day
bridal, bridesmaid
bridegroom a man on his wedding day
bridge something built to cross a river, road or railway
bridges, bridging

arch bridge

beam bridge

suspension bridge
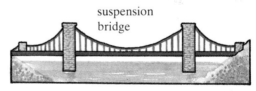

brief short; not taking long
briefly, briefness, brevity
bright 1. giving light; shining
2. clever
brightly, brightness
brilliant very bright
brilliantly, brilliance
bring to carry here
brittle easily broken
broad wide
broadly, broadness, breadth
broadcast to send out a programme on radio or television
broke past tense of 'to break'

23

brooch a decoration to pin on to clothes
brooches
brook a small stream
broom a long-handled brush for sweeping
brother a boy who has the same parents as you
brought past tense of 'to bring'
brown a colour made by mixing red and yellow
bruise a dark mark on the skin made by a hard knock
bruised, bruiser, bruising
brush an instrument for painting, sweeping, or scrubbing
bubble a thin ball of liquid filled with air
bubbling, bubbly, bubbled
bucket a container with a handle, for carrying water
buckle a clasp for fastening a belt or strap
bud a flower or leaf before it opens
budded, budding
budge to move slightly (We pushed hard, but the rock wouldn't budge a millimetre.)
budged, budges, budging
budgerigar a small Australian bird
budgie

buffalo a kind of wild ox
buffaloes
buffer something at the end of a railway line to prevent an engine from being damaged
bugle a musical instrument (See page 90)
bugler
build to put together
builder, building, built
bulb 1. an electric lamp
2. the onion-like root of some plants
bulge a swelling
bulged, bulging, bulges, bulgy
bull a male ox, elephant or whale
bulldog a kind of dog; it is strong and brave
bulldozer a large tractor to move earth
bullet the metal shot from a gun
bullet-proof
bully a person who hurts or frightens those weaker than himself
bullies, bullied, bullying
bumblebee a large kind of bee (See page 18)
bump 1. to knock against something
2. a swelling on the body
bumper, bumpy
bun a small soft cake, usually round

bunch a group of things growing or fastened together
bunches
bundle a collection of things tied together
bundles, bundling
bungalow a house with all its rooms on the one ground floor
bunk 1. a bed in a ship's cabin
2. nonsense
buoy an anchored marker floating on the sea
burglar someone who breaks in to steal
burgle, burgling, burglary
burial the act of burying a dead person

burst to break open suddenly; to explode
bury to put in the ground and cover up
buried, buries, burying, burial
bus a coach for carrying many passengers
buses, busful, bus-conductor, bus stop
busy having much to do
busily, business, busybody
butcher someone who sells meat
butter a yellow dairy food for spreading on bread
buttercup a small yellow flower
butterfly an insect with brightly-coloured wings

swallowtail

painted lady

clouded yellow

scarce copper

large blue

burn 1. to be alight
2. to damage by fire (Don't burn the cakes.)
burner, burnt
burrow a hole in the ground dug and lived in by animals

button a small round object for fastening clothes
buy to get something in exchange for money
buyer, buying, bought
buzz to make a noise like a bee

25

Cc

cabbage a leafy vegetable (See page 151)

cabin 1. a room on a ship or aeroplane
   2. a wooden hut

cable 1. thick strong wire or rope
   2. insulated wire for electricity
   3. a telegram, especially overseas

cactus a prickly desert plant
   cactuses or *cacti*

café a place selling tea, coffee and snacks

cage a box or room with bars for keeping birds or animals

cake a sweet food made with flour and baked in the oven

calculate to find out, especially with maths
   calculating, calculation, calculator

calendar a list of the days, weeks and months

calf 1. a young cow or bull
   2. the back part of your leg
   calves, calving, calved, to calve

call 1. to shout or speak loudly
   2. to visit someone
   3. to name someone (We call him Jim.)
   caller, calling

calm quiet and still; windless
   calmly, calmness, calmer, calmest

calypso a West Indian song

came the past tense of 'to come'

camel a desert animal

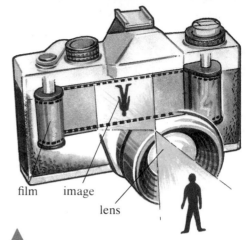

film   image   lens

camera an apparatus for taking photographs

camp 1. a place where tents are set up
   2. to live in tents
   camp-bed, camper, camp-site

can 1. a metal container
   2. to put fruit or vegetables into a can
   3. to be able to; to be allowed to
   cannot, can't, canning, canned

canal a man-made river

canary a yellow bird (See page 20)
   canaries

cancel to cross out; to put a stop to
   cancelled, cancelling, cancellation

candle a stick of wax with a wick in it that gives out light when burning
   candle-light, candlestick

Arabian camel

bactrian camel

cane a stick

cannibal a person who eats human flesh
cannibalism, cannibalistic

cannon a very large heavy gun

canoe a small, narrow boat moved by paddles
canoes, canoeing, canoed

canteen a restaurant for workers

cap a kind of hat, often with a peak

capable able to do something; gifted
capability, capably

capital 1. the chief city (Paris is the capital of France.)
2. a large letter of the alphabet (ABCDE...)

capsize to overturn a boat in the water
capsized, capsizing

captain 1. the leader of a team or group
2. the person in charge of a ship
3. an army or naval officer

captivate to fascinate; to interest greatly
captivated, captivating, captivation

capture to take prisoner
captured, capturing, captive

car a motor vehicle; an automobile

caravan a house on wheels

card a flat piece of stiff paper

cardboard thick card, sometimes in rolls

cardigan a knitted woollen jacket

care 1. to feel interested or to mind
2. to look after
3. caution (Take care! There's a bus coming.)
careful, carefully, careless, careless-ness, carelessly, caring, carefree

caretaker someone who is paid to look after a building such as a school

cargo goods carried on a ship or aircraft
cargoes, cargo-boat

carnival a time for merry-making

carol a song usually sung at Christmas
carol singer

carpenter someone who makes things from wood
carpentry

carpet a floor covering often made of wool

carriage 1. a horse-drawn vehicle
2. a part of a train where people sit

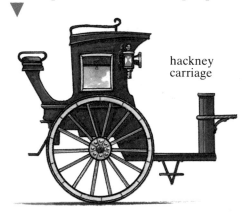

hackney carriage

carrot a root vegetable (See page 151)

carry to take from one place to another
carried, carries, carrying, carrier

cart a vehicle
cart-horse, cart-load, cartwheel

cartoon a drawing that makes fun of something
cartoonist, strip-cartoon

carve 1. to slice meat
2. to cut wood or stone into shapes
carver, carving, carving-knife

case a box with a lid for carrying things

cash money in coins or notes
cash-book, cash-box, cashier

cask a barrel to hold liquids

cassette a plastic container for a tape
cassette-player

cast 1. to throw
2. to mould
3. the actors performing in a play
cast iron, plaster cast, cast off

castle a fortified building with towers

cat a furry pet animal
catty, cattily, cattiness

catalogue a list of things to sell, books, etc.

catapult a weapon for shooting stones

catamaran a boat with two hulls

catch to stop something and grasp it
catchy, catchable, caught, catches

caterpillar the grub of a butterfly or moth

cathedral the chief church of a district

catkin the fluffy flower of the hazel, willow (See page 67)

cattle cows, bulls, and calves

caught the past tense of 'to catch'

cauliflower a vegetable with a flower head

cause 1. to make something happen
2. the reason why something happens
3. a purpose (Helping the old is a good cause.)

caution 1. taking care
2. a warning
cautious, cautiously

cavalry soldiers on horseback

cave a hollow place in rocks
caveman, cavity, cavern, cavernous

caw the cry of a rook or crow

cease to stop
ceaseless, ceaselessly, ceasing, unceasing

cedar an evergreen tree (See page 146)

ceiling the roof of a room

celebrate to do something to show that it is a special day
celebrating, celebrated, celebration, celebrity

celery a vegetable with white stems

cell a small room in a prison or monastery

cellar an underground room

cello a musical instrument of the violin family (See page 90)
cellist

Celsius a temperature scale, also called centigrade

cement a powder used to make concrete

cemetery a burial ground
cemeteries

cent a coin used in many countries

centigrade a scale for measuring temperature, also called Celsius

centimetre one hundredth of a metre

centre the middle point
central, centrally

century 1. a hundred years
2. a hundred runs in cricket
centuries

cereal 1. any food grain
2. a breakfast food made from a cereal

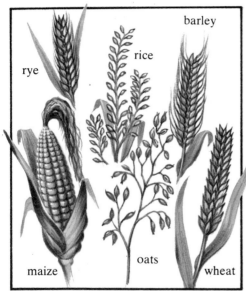

rye

rice

barley

maize

oats

wheat

ceremony a solemn public celebration
ceremonies, ceremonial, ceremonially

certain 1. sure
2. some (person or thing) (Certain children are always late.)
certainly, certainty, uncertain

certificate a piece of paper giving proof of something (Tim has a certificate to show that he can swim ten lengths.)
certify, certified, certifies

chain metal rings joined together

chair a single seat with a back
chairman, chairmen

chalk 1. soft white rock
2. a stick of similar material for writing

challenge to invite someone to a contest (He challenged me to a game of chess.)
challenging, challenger

champion someone who has beaten all others
championship

chance 1. a lucky or unexpected happening (We met quite by chance on the beach.)
2. a possibility (There is no chance of our winning the match.)

change 1. to make something different
2. to become different (The weather has changed; it is fine again.)
changing, changes, changeable, changeless

channel 1. a narrow strip of water
2. a radio or television wavelength

chapel a place of worship

chapter a section of a book

character 1. the qualities that make up the nature of a person
2. a personality (a well-known character)
3. a person in a story or play
characteristic, characterless

charge 1. to ask a price for something
2. to rush forward
charging, charger, chargeable

chariot a horse-drawn vehicle used in ancient times for racing and battle
charioteer

charity 1. kindness; generosity
2. an organisation giving help to the needy
charities, charitable, charitableness

charm 1. to delight or give pleasure
2. a magic spell
charming, charmer, charmingly

chart 1. a map used by sailors
2. a list or diagram giving information (In hospital he had a temperature chart at the foot of his bed.)
charter, chartered, chartering
chase to run after; to pursue
chaser, chasing
chat a friendly talk
chatter, chatted, chatting, chatterbox
chauffeur a person paid to drive someone in a car
cheap costing little money; not dear
cheapness, cheaply, cheapen
cheat to act dishonestly; to trick someone
check 1. to make sure something is right
2. to slow down or stop (He checked his step when he saw the danger.)
3. a pattern of squares
cheek 1. the soft side of your face
2. saucy behaviour; rudeness
cheeky, cheek-bone
cheer 1. to shout in support of someone
2. to make someone happy
cheerful, cheery, cheerfulness, cheerless
cheese a food made from milk
cheetah a fast wild animal of the cat family

chemist 1. an expert in chemistry
2. a person who makes medicines
3. a person who sells medicines, soap, etc.
chemical, chemistry
cheque a signed order to a bank to pay money
cherry a small round fruit with a stone
chess a board game
chessboard, chess-men, chesspieces

king
bishop
rook (castle)
knight
queen
pawn

chest 1. the upper front part of your body
2. a strong box with a lid
chest of drawers, treasure chest
chestnut a tree with brown nuts (See page 144)
chew to crush food with your teeth
chewable, chewing gum
chick a very young bird
chicken 1. a young fowl
2. the meat of hens or cockerels
chickenfeed, chicken-hearted, chickenpox
chief 1. the most important
2. a leader (an Indian chief)
chiefs, chiefly, chieftain
child a young boy or girl
childish, childlike, childhood, children
chill 1. a feeling of coolness
2. an illness

chilly, chilliness

chime the sound made by bells
chiming, chimed

chimney the part of a building that carries smoke away from the fire
chimney-pot, chimney-stack, chimney-sweep

chimpanzee a kind of ape (See page 11)

chin the part of your face below the mouth

china fine cups, saucers and plates made from special white clay

chip a piece cut or broken off
chipped, chipping, chipboard

chirp the short sharp sound made by birds
chirpy, chirpiness

chisel a cutting tool (See page 141)

chocolate a sweet food made from cocoa

choice the right or opportunity to choose

choir a group of people singing together

choke 1. to be unable to breathe properly
2. to block something up
choker, choking

choose to pick out or make a decision
chooses, choosing, chose, chosen, choosy, choice, unchosen

chop 1. to cut with an axe
2. a thick slice of meat with its bone
chopper, chopping, chopped, chopsticks

christen to give a child its Christian name

Christian someone who believes in Jesus Christ
Christianity

Christmas the day celebrating the birth of Christ

chubby plump; rather fat

chuck to throw

chuckle to laugh quietly

chuckling, chuckler

chum a friend
chummy

chunk a large piece (a chunk of bread)
chunky, chunkiness

church a building in which Christians worship
churches, churchyard, churchy

cigar a fat roll of tobacco leaves to smoke

cigarette a small paper-covered roll of tobacco to smoke

cine-camera a camera that takes moving pictures

cinema a place in which films are shown

circle a round flat shape
circular, to circle

▼

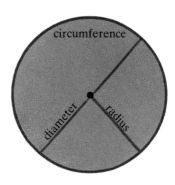

▲

circumference the boundary of a circle

circus a show given by clowns, acrobats and trained animals in a ring

citrus oranges, lemons, limes and grapefruit are citrus fruits

city a very large town
cities, citizen, citizenship

civil 1. to do with citizens
2. polite
civility, civilly, Civil Service, civil war, civilian

civilise to educate and improve
civilised, civilising, civilisation

claim 1. to demand something because

it is yours (She claimed her coat from the Lost Property Office.)
2. to state something as a fact (He claimed that he could swim a mile.)

clap to hit the palms of your hands together
clapped, clapping

clarinet a musical instrument of the woodwind family
clarinettist

clasp to grip firmly

class 1. a group of students who are taught together
2. a group of people or things with something in common
classes, classify, classification

clatter a loud rattling noise

claw a sharp hooked nail on the foot of a bird or other animal

clay a stiff sticky sort of earth used for making bricks and pottery
clayey

clean not dirty; washed
cleaner, cleanliness, cleanly

clear 1. with nothing in the way (We can cross now, as the road is clear.)
2. easy to see or understand (The reason for this is not clear to me.)
3. to go over something without touching
4. to make empty (clear the table)
clearance, clearing,

clergyman a minister in a Christian Church

clerk an office worker
clerical

clever quick to learn; skilful

cliff a very steep hillside, often overlooking the sea

climate the kind of weather a place has

climb to go up, often using hands and feet
climbed, climber, climbing

cling to hold tightly to something
clinger, clinging, clung

clinic a place where doctors and nurses give help or treatment
clinical

clip 1. to fasten together
2. to cut with scissors or shears
clipped, clipper, clipping, paper-clip

cloak a coat that hangs loose from the shoulders
cloakroom

clock an instrument for telling the time
clockwise, clockwork

clog 1. to block up
2. a wooden shoe
clogged, clogging

close 1. near
2. to shut
closed, closing, closure

cloth material woven from wool, cotton, nylon, etc

clothes things to wear
clothed, clothing

cloud a fluffy mass of tiny water-drops floating in the air
cloudy, cloudier, cloudless, cloud-burst

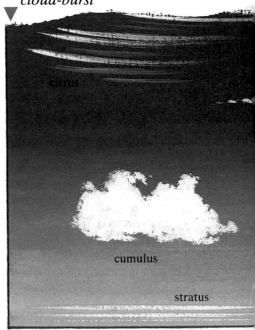

cirrus

cumulus

stratus

white clover

red clover

clover a small wild plant
clown the funny man of a circus
clowning, clownish
club 1. a heavy stick
2. a group of people who meet together
clue something that helps to solve a puzzle
clueless
clumsy awkward
clumsily, clumsiness
coach 1. a bus
2. a horse-drawn carriage
3. a railway carriage
4. an instructor especially in games
coaches

cirrocumulus

cumulonimbus

coal a black substance used for burning
coalfield, coal-mine, coal-scuttle
coarse rough; not smooth or fine
coarsely, coarseness
coast the sea-shore; the land near the sea
coastal, coastline
coat 1. an article of clothing
2. an outer covering
coat-hanger, coating
cobbler a person who mends shoes and boots
cobra a poisonous snake

cobweb a net made by a spider to trap insects
cock a male bird
cockerel, cock-a-doodle-do
cockpit the place for the pilot of an aircraft or the driver of a racing car
cockroach a brown beetle

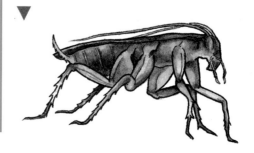

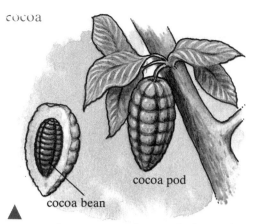

cocoa pod

cocoa bean

cocoa a brown powder made from the beans of the cocoa tree and used for hot drinks

coconut a large brown nut growing on palm trees

cod a large sea fish (See page 55)

code 1. a secret language
2. a set of rules (the Highway Code)

coffee a hot drink made from the roasted beans of the coffee bush

coffin a box in which dead bodies are buried

cog a tooth on a cogwheel

coil to twist into a spiral shape (The sailor coiled the rope on the deck.)

coin a metal disc used as money
coinage

cold 1. low in temperature
2. an illness
cold-blooded, coldly, coldness

collar the part of your clothing that goes round your neck

collect to bring together
collector, collection

college a place where people are taught

collide to bump together by mistake
collided, colliding, collision

colonel a senior army officer

colossal huge; giant-like

colour red and blue are colours
colourful, colouring, colourless

colt a young male horse
coltish

column 1. a post or pillar
2. something that is long and narrow, especially a list of figures or letters

comb an instrument for tidying the hair

combine to join together
combining, combination, combine-harvester

come to move nearer
coming, came

comedian a performer who makes you laugh

comfortable making you free from pain
comfort, comfortably

comic 1. funny
2. a picture paper for young children
comical, comically

comma a punctuation mark (,)

command an order
commander, commando, commandment

commence to begin
commencement, commencing

commit to carry out an action (He committed a crime.)
committed, committing, commitment

committee a group of people formed to organise something

common 1. ordinary, usual
2. shared by others (Two legs are common to birds and humans.)
3. a kind of public park
commonly, commonplace, commonwealth

company 1. being with another person (We kept each other company while waiting.)
2. visitors
3. a business firm
companion, companionship

compare to see if things are alike
comparable, comparing, comparative, comparatively, comparison

compass an instrument showing north, east, south, west

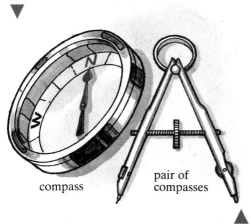

compass   pair of compasses

compasses you draw circles with a pair of compasses

compel to force someone to do something
compelling, compelled, compulsion, compulsory, compulsorily

compete to try to win or do better than others
competing, competition, competitive, competitor

complain to grumble
complaint

complete 1. with nothing missing
2. to finish; to make whole
completely, completing, completion

compose 1. to make up (Our team was composed of two boys and three girls.)
2. to write, especially music
composer, composing, composition

computer a machine that works out very difficult sums or problems

comrade a good friend; a companion
comradely, comradeship

conceal to hide

conceit vanity; feeling too proud
conceited, conceitedly

concern 1. to be of importance to (Road safety concerns us all.)
2. to worry about (Joe's mother was concerned about his bad school report.)

concert a musical performance

concrete a mixture of cement, stones, sand and water that sets like rock

condition 1. a state (in good condition)
2. something that must be done (You can go on condition that you return early.)

conduct 1. behaviour (He was praised for his good conduct.)
2. to guide (He conducted us round the castle.)
conductor, conductress

cone 1. a shape that is round at one end and pointed at the other
2. the fruit of certain evergreen trees
3. an ice-cream cornet
conical

confess to own up; to admit
confesses, confession

confide to tell someone a secret
confiding, confidential
confident feeling sure of oneself
confidence, confidently
confuse to muddle or mix up
confusing, confusion
conjurer someone who does clever
tricks that seem magical
conjure, conjuring
conker the nut of the horse-chestnut
tree
connect to join up
connector, connection
conquer to defeat; to beat in battle
conqueror, conquest

construct to build
*constructor, constructive,
constructively, construction*
contain to hold something inside
container
content satisfied; happy about
something
contented, contentedly, contentment
contents the things inside something
contest a competition or fight
continent one of the large land masses
of the world (Europe, North
America, South America, Asia,
and Africa are all continents.)
continental

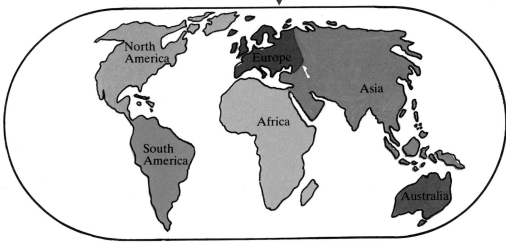

conscience the knowledge of right and
wrong
conscientious, conscientiously
conscious aware of what is happening
consciously, consciousness
consequence something that follows as
a result of something else
consequent, consequently
consider to think about
*considerable, considerably,
consideration*
consonant any letter of the alphabet
except a, e, i, o, u
constable a policeman

continue to go on doing something
*continual, continually,
continuation, continuing,
continuous, continuously*
contribute to give help; to give money
to a cause
*contributing, contributor,
contribution*
control to keep in order
*controls, controlled, controlling,
controller*
convenient handy, suitable and easy to
use
convenience, conveniently

convent a house where nuns live and work

conversation talking with someone
conversational, conversationally

convert to change something into something else (He converted his pounds into francs.)
conversion, convertible

convoy a fleet of ships sailing together for safety

cook to make food ready by heating it
cooker, cookery

cool 1. rather cold
2. calm
coolness, cooler

copper 1. a metal that is reddish brown
2. a policeman (slang)

copy 1. to imitate; to make another the same
2. something made exactly like something else

cord a thin rope

core the central part (an apple core)

cork 1. the bark of the cork-oak tree
2. a piece of cork used as a bottle-stopper
corkscrew

cork oak   cork

corn 1. the seeds of barley, oats, rye and wheat
2. a sore hard lump on your foot

corner 1. where two lines, roads or walls meet
2. a kick from the corner of a football pitch

corpse a dead body

correct right; true
correctly, correction, correctness

corridor a long narrow passage in a building

cosmonaut a Russian spaceman

cost what you have to pay
costly, costliness

costume 1. clothing
2. stage clothes worn by actors

cosy comfortable and warm
cosily, cosiness

cot a baby's bed with sides

cottage a small house, usually in the country

cotton thread made from the cotton plant
cotton-reel, cotton-wool

couch a long soft seat

cough a noisy rush of air from the lungs

could was able to (Liz said she could swim quite well now.)

council a group of people elected to run something, especially a town
councillor

count 1. to say the numbers in order
2. to add up
3. to 'count on' means to rely on
4. to 'count down' means to count backwards
countable, countless

counter 1. a small disc used in games
2. a long table at which customers in a shop or bank are served

country 1. a land where a nation lives
2. the land outside the towns
countryside, countryman, countrified

county one of the large divisions of Great Britain (Devon and Norfolk are counties)

couple a pair; two of anything

coupon a ticket showing your right to something

courage the feeling of not being afraid
courageous, courageously

course 1. a track (a race-course)
2. the direction taken (the course of a ship)
3. a set of lessons
4. a part of a meal (a three course dinner)
5 'of course' means certainly

court 1. an area marked out for playing tennis or other games
2. a place where people are tried for crimes
3. the monarch, family and councillors
courtier, courtyard, courtship

courteous polite and good-mannered
courteously, courteousness, courtesy

cousin the child of your aunt or uncle

cover 1. to put something over something
2. what you put over something to hide it

cow 1. a female ox from which we get milk
2. a female elephant or whale

coward someone who cannot stop himself from being afraid
cowardly, cowardice, cowardliness

cowboy a man who looks after cattle in North America

crab a shelled creature with four pairs of legs and a pair of pincers

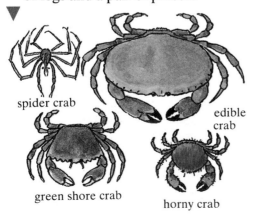

spider crab

edible crab

green shore crab

horny crab

crack 1. a line where something is broken but has not come apart (a crack in a plate)
2. a sharp noise like a pistol going off
3. first-rate (a crack player)

cracker 1. a Christmas plaything that explodes when pulled apart
2. a kind of firework
3. a kind of biscuit

cradle a bed for a young baby

craft 1. a boat or a ship
2. a job needing skilled hands
craftsmanship, craftsman

crane 1. a machine for lifting heavy weights
2. a long-legged bird

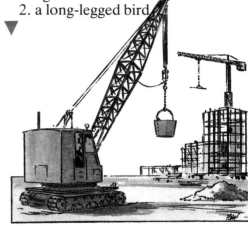

crash 1. a loud noise
2. to hit against something and be smashed
crashes, crash-helmet, crash-landing

crawl 1. to move on hands and knees
2. a stroke in swimming

crayon a coloured wax stick for drawing

craze a short-lived enthusiasm for something
crazy, craziness, crazily

cream the thick part of milk that collects at the top
creamy, creaminess

crease 1. a line caused by folding cloth
2. the line the batsman stands

behind in cricket
creasing, creasible, crease-resisting
create to bring into existence; to make
creation, creator, creative, creatively
creature any living person or animal
credit a person or thing that brings
honour (Tom behaved very wisely
and was a credit to his family.)
creditable, creditably
creek 1. a place where a stream flows
into the sea
2. a stream, in Australia and USA
creep to move very slowly and quietly
creepy, creepiness, crept, creeper
cress a green plant used in salads
crest 1. the top of a hill or wave
2. the bunch of feathers on a bird's
head
3. the official badge of a town,
school, etc.
crew the workers on a ship or aircraft
cricket 1. a team game with bat and
ball
2. an insect
cried the past tense of 'to cry'
crime a serious breaking of the law
criminal, criminally
crimson a deep red colour
crisp hard, dry and easily broken
crisps, crisply, crispness, crispbread
crocodile a large tropical animal

crocus

crocus corm

▲

crocus a small spring flowering corm
crocuses
crook 1. someone who breaks the law
2. a stick with a hook at the end
crooked bent; not straight
crookedly, crookedness
crop plants grown for food
cross 1. to move from one side to the
other
2. a shape like + or X
3. rather angry
*crossly, crossness, cross-bar,
cross-country, cross-eyed, crossfire,
cross-roads, crossword*
crow a large bird with a harsh call (See
page 20)
crowd a great many people all in one
place
crown 1. the head-dress of a king or
queen
2. the top of anything (the crown of
your head, the crown of a hill)

▼

cruel

cruel very unkind; causing pain
cruelly, cruelty
cruise 1. to sail about
2. to travel at the speed that suits a car best
cruiser, cruising, cruise-ship
crumb a tiny piece of bread or cake
crumbly, crumby
crush 1. to press tightly and so damage
2. too many people for comfort
crust the hard outer part of bread
crusty, crustiness
cry 1. to shed tears
2. to call out
cried, crier, cries, crying
cub a young lion, bear, wolf, etc.
cube a solid shape with six equal faces
cubic, cubicle, cubism
cuckoo a bird that lays eggs in other birds' nests

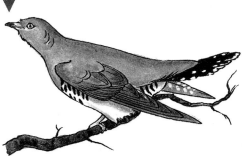

cucumber a long vegetable used in salads
cuddle to hold someone closely and lovingly
cuddlesome, cuddly, cuddling
culprit a person who has done wrong
cultivate to prepare the soil for crops
cultivating, cultivation, cultivator
cunning good at tricking others
cunningly, cunningness
cup a bowl with a handle for drinking
cupful, cupfuls
cupboard a piece of furniture with doors used for storing things
cure 1. to make a sick person better

2. to preserve food by smoking or salting
curable, curing
curious 1. strange, unusual
2. keen to learn about things
curiosity, curiously
curl something twisted into a curve
curly, curliness
currant 1. a small dried grape
2. the fruit of currant bushes
current 1. the flow of air, water or electricity
2. happening now (the current month)
curry food prepared with hot spices
curse to use strong language
curtain cloth hanging down to cover windows
curve a line that is not straight and has no sharp angles
curving, curvature
cushion a cloth bag filled with soft material for a chair
custard sweet sauce made with milk and eggs
custard-powder
custom what usually happens or is done (It's our custom to give Mum breakfast in bed on Sundays.)
customary
customer a person who buys things from a shop
cut to make into smaller pieces with a knife
cutting
cutlery knives, forks and spoons
cycle a bicycle
cycling, cyclist
cyclone a violent storm with strong wind
cylinder an object shaped like a tube
cylindrical
cymbals a pair of plate-shaped musical instruments (See page 90)
cygnet a young swan

Dd

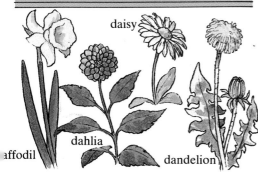

daffodil
daisy
dahlia
dandelion

dab to touch lightly and quickly
dabbed, dabbing

Dad the pet name for a father
daddy, daddies

daffodil a plant that grows from a bulb

dagger a pointed knife used as a weapon

dahlia a garden flower

daily happening every day

dainty pretty and fine
dainties, daintiness, daintily

dairy 1. a place where milk is kept
2. a shop selling milk, butter and cheese
dairies, dairy-farm, dairyman, dairymaid

daisy a common flower

dam a wall built to hold back water

damage to harm or cause loss of value
damaging

damp slightly wet
dampen, dampening

dance to move around in time to music
dancer, dancing

dandelion a wild flower and weed

danger something that can kill or harm
dangerous, dangerously

dare 1. to have the courage to do something
2. to challenge someone to do something (I dare you to jump off that rock.)
daring, daringly

dark 1. having little or no light
2. deep in colour (dark blue)
darkish, darkly

darling someone you love very much

darn to mend a hole in clothes

dart 1. to move quickly and suddenly
2. a small arrow for throwing

dash 1. to move fast and hurriedly
2. a short line for punctuation (—)

date 1. the day, month and year
2. a meeting arranged between two people
3. the fruit of the palm-tree
dated, dating

daughter someone's girl child
daughter-in-law, daughters-in-law

dawn first light; day-break

day 1. a period of 24 hours
2. not night; between sunrise and
sunset
day-break, daylight, day-time, daily

dazed too stunned to know what you
are doing

dazzle to blind briefly with bright light
dazzled, dazzling

dead without life; no longer living
deaden, deadly, death, deathly

deaf unable to hear
deafen, deafness, deafening

deal 1. to give out (You deal the
cards.)
2. to do business with someone
3. to take action (I will deal with the
problem.)
dealer, dealt

dear 1. costing a lot of money
2. loved very much by someone
dearest, dearly

debt money you owe to someone

decay to go bad; to rot

deceive to make someone believe what
you know to be untrue
*deceit, deceitful, deceitfully,
deceiving, deceptive*

December the twelfth month of the
year

decent 1. pleasant or good enough
2. proper; modest
decently, decency

decide to make up your mind
deciding, decision, decisive

decimal having to do with tens or
tenths
decimal point, decimalisation

deck a floor or ceiling on a ship or
aircraft
deck-chair

declare 1. to say something very
definitely
2. to close the innings in cricket
declaration, declaring

decline 1. to say no to an invitation
2. to become weaker or less
declined, declining

decorate 1. to make something look
prettier
2. to give someone a medal
*decoration, decorating, decorative,
decoratively, decorator*

decrease to become smaller
decreasing

deduct to take away; to subtract
deduction

deed something which has been done
(a good deed)

deep a long way down
deeply, deepen, depth

deer a fast-running animal with antlers

chinese water
deer (doe)

sika deer
(stag)

red deer
(stag)

fallow deer
(stag)

defeat to beat someone in a game or contest

defend to guard; to keep safe from danger
defence, defenceless, defensive

definite sure, certain
definitely, definition, definiteness

defy to resist boldly and openly
defied, defies, defying, defiance

delay to make someone or something late

deliberate done on purpose
deliberately

delicate 1. soft, tender, fine
2. easily becoming ill (a delicate child)
delicately, delicacy, delicacies

delight great pleasure or joy
delightful, delightfully

deliver to take to a place (Please deliver the parcel.)
delivery

demand to ask for

demolish to pull down or destroy
demolition

demon an evil spirit; a devil

demonstrate 1. to show how something is done
2. to go in procession to demand something
demonstration, demonstrator, demonstrating

den the home of certain wild animals

dense very thick; stupid
densely, density, denseness

dent to make a hollow in a flat surface

dentist someone who looks after your teeth
dental, dentistry

deny to say that something is not true
denied, denies, denial, denying

depart to go away; to leave
departure

depend to rely on
dependable, dependent, dependant

deposit 1. to put down and leave
2. money left in part payment
deposited, depositing

depth the distance from top to bottom

derail to make a train go off the rails

derrick 1. a large crane
2. a tower over an oil well

drill

descend to go down or come down
descendant, descent

describe to give a picture of something in words
describing, description, descriptive

desert a large area of land that gets little or no rain

deserve to earn something by doing well
deserved, deserving

design 1. a pattern
2. a plan for building
designer

desire to want something very much
desirable, desirability, desiring

desk a table for writing or reading

destroy to wreck; to make useless
destroyer, destruction, destructive

detail a small part or item

detect to discover; to find out
detection, detective, detector

detergent a household cleaner
determined with your mind firmly made up
determination, determinedly
detest to hate; to dislike very much
detestable, detestation
develop to make or become bigger or better
developing, developed, development
devise to make for a special purpose
devising, device
devil a wicked spirit
devilish, devilment, devilry
dew drops of water that settle on the ground during the night
dewdrop, dewy
diagram a drawing to explain something
dial 1. a flat face with numbers on it
2. to telephone by turning the dial
dialled, dialling
dialect the form of language used in a particular district of a country
dialogue a conversation
diamond a very hard precious stone
diary a notebook in which you can write about what you do every day
diaries
dictate 1. to tell others what to do
2. to speak to someone who writes down your words
dictating, dictation, dictator

dictionary a book giving the meanings of words
dictionaries
die to stop living
died, dies, dying
diesel an engine burning a special oil
diet 1. the food you normally eat
2. the food you eat for medical reasons, for example, to lose weight
dietetic, dietician
differ not to be the same as
different, difference, differing, differred
difficult hard to do; not easy
dig to turn over the soil with a spade
digger, digging, dug
digest when you digest food the stomach changes it so that the body can take the goodness from it
digestion, digestive, digestible
dim not bright; difficult to see
dimmer, dimmest, dimly
din a loud noise that continues
dine to eat dinner
diner, dining-room
dinghy a small rowing boat
dinner the main meal of the day
dinosaur huge reptiles that lived in very early times

Stegosaurus

dip 1. to make lower (Dip your
  headlights.)
  2. to put into liquid for a short time
  3. to slope downwards
  dipped, dipper, dipping
direct 1. to show someone the way
  2. straight; by the shortest way
  direction, directly, director
directory a book containing lists of
  names (a telephone directory)
dirty not clean; needing to be washed
  dirtier, dirtiest, dirtily, dirtiness
disagree to think differently; to differ
  *disagreeable, disagreeably, disagree-
  ment*
disappear to go out of sight; to vanish
  disappeared, disappearance
disappoint to make someone sad by
  not doing what had been hoped
  disappointing, disappointment
disarm to take weapons away from
  people
  disarmament, disarming

disaster a serious accident or
  misfortune
  disastrous, disastrously
disc 1. something round and flat
  2. a record
  disc jockey
disciple a follower of a great person
discipline well-trained behaviour
  disciplined, disciplinarian
discover to find something out
  discoverer, discovery
discuss to talk about something
  discussed, discussion
disease an illness; sickness
disgrace shame
  disgraceful, disgracefully
disguise to change your appearance in
  order to deceive people
dish 1. a plate or bowl for food
  2. a particular food (a tasty dish)
  dishful, dish-cloth, dish-water
dishonest not to be trusted; not honest
  dishonestly, dishonesty
dislike not to like
disloyal letting someone down; not
  loyal
dismiss to send away; to cease to
  employ
  dismissed, dismissal
disobey not to do what one is told
  *disobedience, disobedient,
  disobediently*

Atlantosaurus

Tyrannosaurus rex

Triceratops

45

disorder confusion
disorderly, disorderliness
display to show so as to be easily seen
disqualify to say something is not fit
disqualified, disqualification
dissolve to mix something with liquid
so as to become liquid itself
distance the space between two places
distant, distantly
distinct easily seen or heard; clear
distinction, distinctly, distinctive
distress great sorrow or unhappiness
distribute to share out; to give out
distributing, distribution
district a part of a town or country
disturb to spoil someone's rest or quiet
disturbance
ditch a long narrow hole for water
ditches

dive to jump into water head first
diving, diver
divide 1. to separate into smaller parts
2. to see how often one number goes
into another (Ten divided by two
equals five.)
dividing, division, divisible
divine like God; perfect
divinely, divinity
dizzy feeling giddy
dock a place where ships are loaded
and unloaded
docker, dockyard
doctor a person trained to look after
your health
dodge to move quickly out of the way
dodgem, dodger, dodging
dog a barking animal often kept as a
pet

pointer

keeshond

setter

elkhound

poodle

great dane

mastiff

spaniel

alsatian

collie

dalmatian

doll a toy model of a real person
dollar a unit of money
dolphin a sea animal like a small whale
domestic to do with the home
    domesticated, domesticity
domino a small brick-like part of a
    game
    dominoes
donkey an animal that brays

door something to open to enter a
    room
    door-bell, door-mat, doorway
dose an amount of medicine
double 1. to make twice as big
    2. to fold into two
    doubled, doubling, double-barrelled
doubt to be unsure about something
    doubtful, doubtfully, doubtless
dough a thick floury mixture for
    making bread or buns
    doughnut, doughy
dove a kind of pigeon (See page 20)
down at or to a lower place
    downcast, downfall, down-hearted,
    downhill, downstairs, downward
dozen a set of twelve
drag to pull something along
    dragged, dragging
dragon a frightening fire-breathing
    monster in stories

dried

dragonfly an insect
    with two pairs of wings
drain a pipe to run off waste water
    drainage, drain-pipe,
    draining-board
drama 1. a play
    2. an exciting event
    dramatic, dramatically, dramatist
draper a person who sells things made
    of cloth
draught a stream of air
    draughty, draughtier, draughtiest
draughts a game played with counters
draw 1. to use a pencil to make a
    picture
    2. to move (As we drew nearer, we
    saw what had happened.)
    3. neither side having won or lost
    (The match ended in a draw.)
    drawback, drawbridge,
    drawing-board, drawing-pin,
    drawing-room, drew
drawer a kind of tray that slides in and
    out of a piece of furniture
dread a great fear
    dreadful, dreadfully
dream what you seem to see in your
    sleep
    dreamy, dreaminess, dreamily
drench to make wet through
dress 1. to put clothes on
    2. an outer garment worn by girls
    dressing-table, dressing-gown,
    dressmaker
drew past tense of 'to draw'
dried past tense of 'to dry'

drill 1. a tool for making holes
    2. any exercise repeated often
drink to swallow liquid
    drank, drinkable, drinker, drunk
drip to fall in drops
    dripped, dripping, drip-dry
drive 1. to make a machine go
    2. a road leading to a large house
    3. to force along
    driven, driver, driving, drove
drizzle fine misty rain
    drizzling, drizzly
drone 1. to make a low humming noise
    2. a male bee
drop 1. to let something fall
    2. a small spot of liquid
    dropped, dropping
drove past tense of 'to drive'
drown to die under water

bass drum

side drum

kettle drum

drum 1. a musical instrument for beating
    2. a container shaped like a cylinder
dry without water; not wet
    drier, driest, drily, drying, dryness
duchess the wife of a duke

tufted duck

teal

mallard

duck a water bird
due 1. owing
    2. expected (The train is due at 10.12.)
    duly
duel a fight between two people with guns or swords
duet music played or sung by two people
duffel-coat a heavy coat with a hood
duke a nobleman of the highest rank
dull 1. not interesting, boring
    2. not bright
    dully, dullness
dumb unable to speak
    dumbfounded, dumbly
dungeon an underground prison
duplicate to make an exact copy
during while something lasts
dusk the dim light before sunset
dust tiny specks of dry dirt
    dustbin, dusty, dustier, dustiness
duster a cloth for removing dust
duty what you ought to do
    duties, dutiful, dutifully
duvet a thick light bed covering
dwarf a very small person
dwell to live somewhere
    dweller, dwelling
dye to colour material by dipping
    dyeing, dyed, dyed-in-the-wool
dying from 'to die'

Ee

each every one of a small set
eager wanting something very much
  eagerly, eagerness
eagle a large soaring bird (See page 21)
ear 1. the part of the head for hearing
  2. the seeds on a stalk of corn
  ear-ache, ear-phone, ear-ring,
  earshot

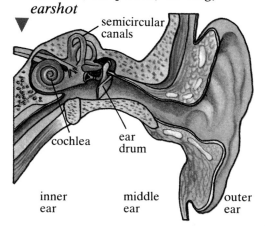

semicircular canals

cochlea
ear drum

inner ear
middle ear
outer ear

earl a nobleman of high rank
early 1. before the right time
  2. a long time ago (in the early days)
  earlier, earliest, earliness
earn to get something by working
  earned, earnings
earnest determined; serious
  earnestly, earnestness
earth 1. the world where we live
  2. the soil we plant things in
  earthen, earthly, earthliness, earthy
earthquake a sudden strong shaking of
  the earth
earwig a small insect (See page 73)
easel a stand to hold a blackboard or a
  painting
east a direction; one of the four points
  of the compass
  easterly, eastern, eastward

Easter the time when Christians
  celebrate the rising of Jesus from
  the dead
easy simple; not hard
  easier, easiest, easily, easiness
eat to take food and swallow it
  ate, eatable, eaten, eater
echo a sound that is repeated because
  it bounces back from something
  echoed, echoes, echoing
eclipse a time when the moon comes
  between the earth and the sun and
  blocks its light

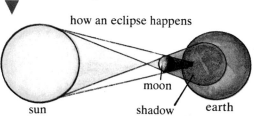

how an eclipse happens

moon

sun   shadow   earth

edge the border or limit of something
educate to teach or train someone
  educating, education, educational
eel a long fish like a snake (See page
  55)
effect the result
  effective, effectively, effectiveness
efficient doing the work well
  efficiently, efficiency
effort hard work; a good try
egg an oval object laid by birds, insects
  and reptiles from which their young
  hatch out
  egg-cup, egg-shell, egg-spoon
eight the number 8
  eighth
eighteen the number 18
  eighteenth
eighty the number 80
  eighty-one, eighties, eightieth
either one or the other of two things
eject to throw out
elastic a material that stretches and
  goes back to its own length

elbow the joint where the arm bends
elder 1. older
   2. a tree (See page 145)
   elderly, eldest
elect to choose by voting
   election, electorate
electricity power supplied by cable
   electric, electrical, electrically,
   electrician, electrify, electrification
elephant the largest land animal

African
elephant

Indian
elephant

eleven the number 11
   eleventh
elm a large tree
elevator 1. a lift
   2. a high building to store grain
else as well (Does anyone else want
   one?)
   elsewhere
embankment 1. a wall to strengthen a
   river bank
   2. a bank built to carry a road or
   track

emerald a bright green precious stone
emerge to come out into the open
   emerging, emergency, emergencies
emigrate to go to live in another
   country
   emigrating, emigrant, emigration
emperor the ruler of an empire
empire a group of countries ruled by
   one person
employ to give work to people and pay
   them
   employee, employer, employment
empress the female ruler of an empire
   or the wife of an emperor
empty with nothing inside
   empties, emptied, emptiness,
   emptying

emu a large Australian bird
enable to make something possible
   (The money enabled me to buy it.)
   enabled, enabling
encourage to help by giving hope
   encouragement, encouraging,
   encouragingly
encyclopaedia a book with
   information about many subjects,
   usually arranged alphabetically
end the finish; the last part of
   something

enemy someone who hates you and wishes to harm you
enemies

energy strength; power
energetic, energetically

engine a machine that powers something

engineer 1. someone who designs machines
2. someone who looks after machines

enjoy to like doing something
enjoyable, enjoyment, enjoyably

enormous very large
enormously, enormousness, enormity

enter to go in
entrance, entry, entrant

enough as many or as much as is needed

entertain 1. to amuse and make people happy
2. to invite people to eat at your house
entertainer, entertainment, entertainingly

entire whole; complete
entirely, entirety

envelope a paper wrapper for a letter

envy a jealous feeling of wanting what someone else has
envious, enviously, envied, envies, envying

equal the same in number of size
equality, equalize, equalizer, equalizing, equalling, equally

equator a line that you can imagine going round the centre of the earth
equatorial

errand a short journey to do something for someone

error a mistake

escalator a moving staircase

escape to get away; to become free
escaping, escaped

Eskimo a member of a race living far north in America and Greenland

essential very necessary

especially for a particular person or thing (I have made this cake especially for you.)

estimate to guess the size or value
estimation

etcetera and other things like them; and so on
(usually shortened to etc.)

eternal never ending; lasting for ever
eternally, eternity

eucalyptus gum tree (See page 145)

even 1. level; smooth
2. not odd in number (An even number can be divided exactly by two: 2, 4, 6, etc.)
evenly, evenness

evening the time between the afternoon and night

event a happening

ever 1. at any time (Do you ever play?)
2. always (He has given up smoking for ever.)
evergreen, everlasting, evermore

every each; all
everybody, everyone, everything, everywhere

evil wicked; sinful
evilly, evil-minded

evolve to develop gradually
evolution, evolutionary, evolving

ewe a female sheep

exact perfectly correct
exactly, exactness

exaggerate to say that something is bigger or better than it really is
exaggeration, exaggerating

examine to test; to look at carefully
examination, examiner, examining

example something that shows what the others in a set are like (This is an example of Tom's painting.)

excavate to dig out

excavation, excavating, excavator
excellent very good
  excellence, excellently
except leaving out (all except one)
exchange to change one thing for
  another
excite to stir up someone's feelings
  excitable, excitement, exciting
exclaim to shout out
  exclamation, exclamation mark
excursion an outing or journey
excuse a reason for not doing something
  excusable, excusably, excusing
execute to kill a person officially as
  punishment
  execution, executioner, executing
exercise 1. a task to give practice
  2. moving the body to keep fit
  exercising
exhaust 1. to use up all energy or
  supplies
  2. a pipe to let out engine fumes
  exhausting, exhaustion, exhaustive
exhibit 1. to put something on show
  2. something that is put on show
  exhibited, exhibition
exile to send someone away from their
  country as punishment
exist to live; to be real
  existence
exit the way out
expand to grow larger
  expansion, expanse, expansive

expect to think something will happen
  expectant, expectation, expectantly
expedition a special journey to find
  something out
expel to drive out; to send away
  expelled, expelling, expulsion
expense the cost of things
  expensive, expenditure
experiment a trial to see what happens
  experimental
expert very skilful
  expertly, expertness, expertise
explain to make the meaning clear
  explanation, explanatory
explode to burst with a big bang
  exploding, explosion, explosive
explore to search unknown places to
  find out more about them
  exploring, exploration, explorer
export to send goods to be sold abroad
  exporter, exportable
express 1. to speak or write clearly
  2. a very fast train
  expression, expressionless,
  expressive
extra more than usual
extraordinary very unusual or
  surprising
  extraordinarily, extraordinariness
extreme not moderate; strong
  extremely
eye the part of the body for seeing
  eyeball, eyebrow, eyelash, eyelid,
  eyesight, eyesore, eye-shadow

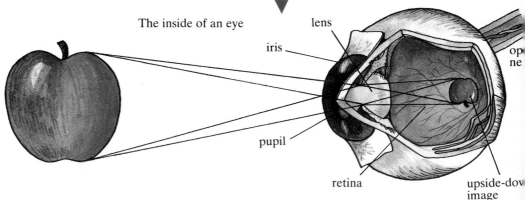

The inside of an eye

lens
iris
op
ne
pupil
retina
upside-dov
image

Ff

fable a short animal story told to teach a lesson

fabulous happening only in stories; wonderful

face the front part of the head

fact something that is true
factual

factory a building where things are made by machine
factories

fade to lose colour
faded, fading

fail to try unsuccessfully to do something
failure

faint 1. not easy to see; weak .
2. to become unconscious from weakness
faint-hearted, faintly, faintness

fair 1. light in colour (fair-haired)
2. keeping to the rules (A referee must always be fair to both sides.)
3. half way between good and bad
4. a place of amusement
fair-ground, fairly, fairness

fairy a small magical person in stories
fairies, fairy-tale, fairyland

faith strong belief
faithful, faithfully, faithfulness

fake something that is not what it is made out to be

fall to drop down
fallen, falling, fell

false 1. not true
2. imitating the real thing
falsehood, falsely, falseness, falsify

familiar known

family a father, mother, and their children
families

famine a great shortage of food

famous well known for something good

fan 1. something to make a breeze
2. a keen supporter (a football fan)
fanned, fanning

electric fan

fan

fang a long pointed tooth

far a long way off

fare money paid by a passenger

farewell good-bye

farm 1. the house where a farmer lives
2. land where food is grown or animals kept
farmhouse, farming, farmyard

farther at a greater distance
farthest

fashion the style of clothes and other things that are popular at a particular time
fashionable, fashionably, unfashionable

fast 1. quick
2. to go without food
3. fixed (The rope held the boat fast.)
fasten, fastener

fat 1. the white greasy part of meat
2. having too much fat; plump
fatten, fatter, fattest, fatness, fatty

fate what is bound to happen
fatal, fatally, fatality, fatalities

father a male parent
fatherhood, fatherless, fatherly

fathom a unit for measuring water — nearly two metres

fault something which is not as it should be
faulty, faultily, faultiness

favourite a person or thing liked best
favourable, favouritism, favour

fawn a young deer

fear a feeling of being in danger
fearful, fearfully, fearless, fearlessly, fearfulness, fearsome

feast a large meal for many people

feat something done bravely or cleverly

feather one of the light plumes on a bird's skin
feathery

February the second month of the year

fee money paid for a professional job

feeble very weak
feebleness, feebly

feed 1. to give food to
2. to eat
feeder, feeding-bottle

feel 1. to touch
2. to be aware of being touched
3. to think (I feel that this is right.)
feeler, feelings, felt

feet more than one foot

fell 1. past tense of 'to fall'
2. to cut down (to fell trees)

female 1. the opposite of male
2. a girl or a woman

fence posts or wire round a field or garden

fern a plant with feathery leaves and no flowers

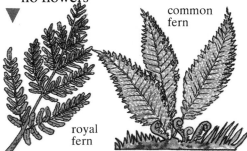

common fern

royal fern

ferry a boat to carry cars or people across water
ferries, ferried

fertile producing good crops
fertility, fertilize, fertilizer

festival a time of celebration with feasting

fetch to go and get

fever an illness making the body hot
feverish, feverishly, feverishness

few not many

fibre a fine thread
fibrous, fibreglass

fiction something made up; stories

fiddle 1. to play a violin
2. to fidget
3. to cheat
fiddler, fiddling

fidget to move about restlessly
fidgety, fidgetiness, fidgeter

field a piece of land, often with grass

fiend a devil or evil spirit
fiendish, fiendishly, fiendishness

fierce wild and angry
fiercely, fierceness

fifteen the number 15
fifteenth

fifty the number 50
fiftieth, fifty-fifty

fight to struggle with someone; to battle
fighter, fought

figure 1. a number
2. the shape of a body
3. a diagram

file 1. a smoothing tool (See page 141)
2. a line of people one behind the other
3. a box or folder to keep papers in

fill to make something full
filler, filling station

filly a young female horse
fillies

film 1. a moving picture
2. the material for taking photo-

graphs

filthy very dirty
filthily, filthiness, filth

fin the part of a fish used for swimming

final at the end; coming last
finalist, finality, finally, finalize

find to come across what has been lost
finder, found, findings

fine 1. dry and sunny (a fine day)
2. very thin like a thread
3. money paid as a punishment
4. in good health (I'm fine, thank you.)

finger a part of the hand
finger-nail, finger-tip, finger-print

finish to end something

fir an evergreen tree with cones (See page 146)

fire 1. something that is burning
2. to shoot a gun
fire-alarm, fire-brigade, fire-engine, fire-escape, fire-extinguisher, fire-light, fireman, fireplace, fireproof, fireside

fireworks small explosives that burn attractively or noisily

firm 1. fixed; steady
2. a business
firmly, firmness

first before all else
firstly, first-aid

fish a swimming animal that lives in water
fisherman, fishing-boat, fishing-line, fishing-net, fishing-rod, fishmonger

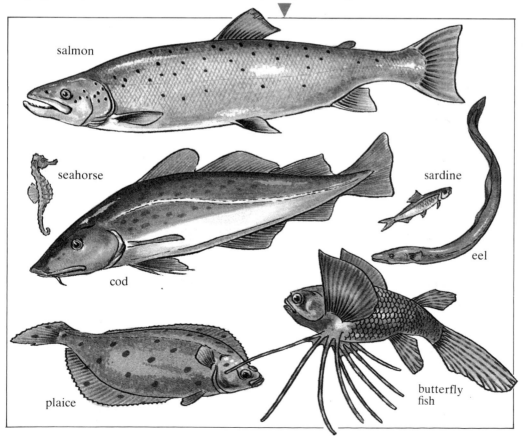

salmon

seahorse

cod

plaice

sardine

eel

butterfly fish

fist a tightly closed hand
fit 1. feeling well and healthy
   2. to be the right size and shape
   3. good enough (The shirt isn't fit to wear.)
   fitted, fitting, fittingly, fitter
five the number 5
   fifth, fiver
fix 1. to make something firm
   2. to mend or arrange something
   fixer, fixture
flag a piece of cloth with a pattern on it used as a sign
   flagged, flagging, flag-pole, flagship

   2. a set of rooms on one floor
   flatter, flattest, flatly, flatten
flavour the taste of something
flee to run away in fear
   fled
fleece a sheep's woolly coat
   fleeced, fleecy
fleet 1. many ships or aeroplanes going together
   2. fast
flesh the soft part of the body between skin and bones
flew the past tense of 'to fly'
flexible easily bent

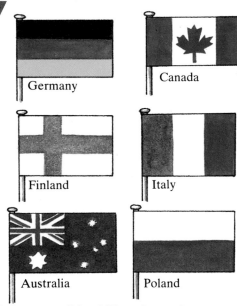

Germany Canada Finland Italy Australia Poland

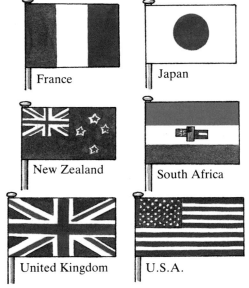

France Japan New Zealand South Africa United Kingdom U.S.A.

flake a small leaf-like piece of something (snow-flakes, soap-flakes)
flame a tongue of fire
   flame-thrower
flannel 1. a soft kind of cloth
   2. a piece of cloth for washing the face
flap to move up and down like wings
   flapped, flapping
flash a sudden brief burst of light
flask a kind of bottle
flat 1. smooth and level

flies 1. present tense of 'to fly' (That pilot flies a jumbo jet.)
   2. the plural of 'a fly'
flight 1. the act of flying
   2. a running away
fling to throw something
   flung
flint a very hard stone
flipper 1. the fin-like limb of a sea animal
   2. a device to help you swim faster
float to rest on the surface of water

flock a large group of birds or animals

flog to beat hard with a stick
flogged, flogging

flood water overflowing from a river or the sea

floor the part of a building to walk on
floor-board, ground floor

florist someone who sells flowers in a shop

flour a white powder made from grain such as wheat and used for cooking

flow to move along like river water

flower the part of a plant with coloured petals that makes the seeds
flower-bed, flower-pot, flowery

flu short for influenza, a fever

fluff soft woolly stuff
fluffy

flute a musical instrument (See page 90)
fluting, flautist

fly 1. to move through the air
2. a small winged insect (See page 73)
flew, flies, flown, flyer, fly-over, fly-wheel

foal a young horse

foam froth on the top of water
foam-rubber, foamy, foaminess

fog thick mist in dirty air
foggy, fogginess

fold to double something over
folder

folk people
folk-dance, folk-song

follow 1. to go after
2. to understand

fond loving; keen

food anything that can be eaten

fool someone who behaves stupidly
foolish, foolishly, foolproof

foot 1. the part of the body you walk on
2. a unit of length, about 30 cm
football, footballer, footlights, foot-path, footstep, footwear, feet

forbid to order someone not to do something
forbade, forbidden, forbidding

force 1. the use of strength
2. to make someone do something
forceful, forcefully, forcing

fore the front (to the fore)
foreground, forehead, forefathers, foreman, foremost, foresee, fore-sight, foretaste, foretell, forethought

forecast to say something will happen before it actually happens

forecastle or **fo'c'sle** the raised deck at the bow of a ship

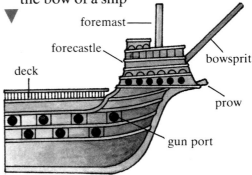

foreign belonging to another country
foreigner

forest land covered with trees
forester, forestry

forget to let something escape your memory
forgetful, forgetfully, forgetfulness, forgetting, forgotten

forgive to stop being angry with someone
forgiveness, forgiving, forgiven

fork 1. a tool with prongs for eating or gardening
2. a place where two roads branch

form 1. the shape of something
2. a kind of bench
3. a class in school
4. a printed paper with spaces to fill
formal, formality, formation, formless

former the first of two things just
mentioned
formerly

fort a building with strong walls to
keep out the enemy
*fortification, fortify, fortified,
fortress*

fortnight two weeks

fortune 1. good or bad luck
2. a large sum of money
fortunate, fortunately, fortune-teller

forty the number 40
fortieth, forty-five

forward to the front
forwardness

fossil the remains of a prehistoric
animal or plant that has been turned
to stone
fossilized

ammonite   trilobite

fought the past tense of 'to fight'

found 1. the past tense of 'to find'
2. to begin the building of something (This college was founded in
1834.)
foundation, founder

foundry a place where metal or glass is
melted and formed into shapes

fountain water shooting up into the air

four the number 4
fourth, fourthly

fourteen the number 14
fourteenth

fowl an old-fashioned word for a bird,
particularly a chicken

female fox
(vixen)

fox cub

fox a wild animal with a long bushy tail
foxes, foxhound, foxy

fraction a part of a whole, e.g. a
quarter

fracture a crack, usually of a bone

fragile delicate; easily broken

fragment a small bit of something that
has broken

fragrant sweet smelling

frame 1. an edging for a picture
2. joined bars used as a support
framework, framed, framing

free 1. to be had without payment
2. able to do what you want to
freedom, freely

freeze to turn into ice
freezer, freezing, froze, frozen,

frequent happening often
frequency, frequently

fresh 1. newly made; not tired
2. different (a fresh sheet of paper)
freshen, freshly, freshness

Friday the sixth day of the week

fridge short for 'refrigerator'

fried the past tense of 'to fry'

friend someone you know and like
friendliness, friendly, friendship

fright sudden fear
frighten, frightful, frightfully

frock a dress worn by a girl or woman

tree frog

reed frog

Common frog

strawberry frog

frog a small jumping animal
front 1. the part that faces forward
2. farthest forward (the front seats)
frost frozen mist or dew
frostbite, frostbitten, frosty, frostiness
froth tiny bubbles on top of water
frown to crease your forehead because you are angry or puzzled
frozen the past tense of 'to freeze'
fruit the part of a plant that holds the seeds
fruitful, fruitless, fruity

fry to cook in hot fat or oil
fried, fries, frying-pan, fryer
fuel anything to burn to make heat
fulfil to carry out what you are expected to do or have promised to
fulfilled, fulfilling, fulfilment
full not able to hold anything more
fullness, full stop, fully
fun enjoyment; being happy
funny, funnily
fund money collected for a special purpose
funeral the ceremony when a dead person is buried or cremated
funnel 1. the chimney of a ship
2. a device to help pour liquid into narrow openings
fur the soft hair that covers some animals
furred, furry
fury great anger
furious, furiously
furnace a special fire-place for making great heat
furnish to put furniture into a room
furnished, furnishes
furniture tables, chairs, beds, etc.
further 1. at a greater distance; farther
2. in addition; additional (Can you give me further details?)
furthermore, furthermost, furthest

peaches

plums

pear

apple

water melon

pineapple

lemon

bananas

raspberries

orange

strawberries

59

fuse 1. a safety device in electrical systems
2. a device for setting off an explosive
fused, fusing, fuses
fuselage the body of an aeroplane
future the time still to come

Gg

gadget any useful tool or piece of machinery
gag to stop someone's mouth
gagged, gagging
gaily in a gay way; cheerfully
gain to get something; to earn or win
galaxy a group of stars
gale a very strong wind
gallant 1. brave
2. very polite to ladies
gallantly, gallantry
galleon a large Spanish sailing ship

gallery a room for the display of art
galley 1. a boat rowed by slaves
2. a ship's kitchen
gallon measure for liquids; 4.5 litres
gallop to run like a horse at its fastest
galloped, galloping
gamble to play games for money
gambling, gambler
game 1. something played to rules
2. animals or birds hunted for food or sport
gamekeeper
gander a male goose
gang a set of people working together
gangway 1. a way between two rows of seats
2. a movable bridge between ships and shore
gaol a prison; a jail
gaoler
gap an opening; a space between two things
garage 1. a place where cars are kept
2. a place where cars are repaired

galleons in battle

garden a piece of land for growing flowers, fruit or vegetables
gardener, gardening

garment any piece of clothing

gas anything not solid or liquid like air
gas-fire, gas-ring, gas-works, gases, gassed

gasp to take a quick deep breath

gate a kind of door in a wall, hedge or fence
gatepost, gateway

gather 1. to collect or bring together
2. to understand (I gather you are his sister.)

gay happy and full of fun
gaiety, gaily

gaze to look at steadily for a long time
gazing

gazelle a small fast antelope

gear 1. a mechanism for controlling speed
2. clothes or things needed for a special purpose
gear-box, gear-lever

geese the plural of 'goose'

gem a precious stone; anything very beautiful

general 1. concerning everyone (general knowledge)

2. not detailed (a general idea)
3. an army officer of high rank
generally

generous ready to give freely
generosity, generously

gentle not rough; quiet and kind
gently, gentleness

gentleman a polite word for 'man'

geography the study of the earth and its people
geographical, geographer

germ a tiny living thing seen only under a microscope

get to obtain; to fetch
getting, got

ghost the spirit of a dead person when it seems to appear to a living person
ghostly, ghostliness

giant a huge person or thing
gigantic, gigantically

giddy a feeling that everything is going round
giddier, giddiest, giddily, giddiness

gift 1. a present
2. a special ability

gill an opening through which a fish breathes

ginger 1. a hot spicy flavouring
2. a reddish yellow colour (ginger hair)
ginger beer, gingerbread, gingery, gingerly

gipsy people that wander from place to place, often in caravans
gipsies

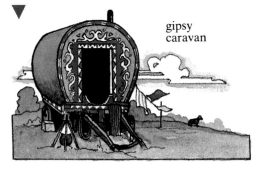

gipsy caravan

giraffe an African animal with a long neck

girl a female child
girl-friend, girlhood, girlish

give to hand over
gave, given, giver, giving

glacier a slow-moving river of ice

glad happy; pleased
gladly, gladness

glance a quick short look
glancing

glare 1. to stare angrily
2. to dazzle
glaring

glass 1. hard material that you can see through
2. a tumbler made of glass
looking-glass, glasses, glassy

glide to move smoothly through air or water
glider, gliding

glimpse a brief look

glitter to sparkle; to shine brightly

globe anything shaped like a ball
global

gloom sadness; misery
gloomy, gloomier, gloomiest, gloominess

glory splendid fame
glorious, gloriously

glove a covering for the hand

glow to shine
glow-worm

glue something to stick things together
gluing, glued, gluey, glueyness

glutton a very greedy person
gluttonous, gluttony

gnat a small flying insect that bites

gnaw to keep on biting something

gnome an imaginary underground dwarf

gnu another name for the wildebeest (See page 156)

go to leave; to move
goes, going, gone, went

goal 1. something you aim for
2. a point scored in football
goal-keeper, goal-post

goat an animal with horns and a beard

gobble to eat quickly and greedily
gobbled, gobbling, gobbler

god someone or something worshipped
godfather, god-like, god-mother, godly

goddess a female god

goggles spectacles worn to protect the eyes

gold a very precious yellow metal

goldfish a small yellowish-red fish

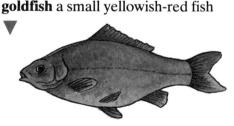

golf an outdoor game played with clubs

golliwog a black-faced doll

gondolier
gondola

gondola a long narrow boat used on canals in Venice
gondolier
gone from the verb 'to go' (He has gone home.)
good 1. of high quality
2. well behaved
goodness, better, best
goodbye what you say when going away
goose a large water bird
geese, gooseflesh, gosling

white-fronted goose

barnacle goose

gooseberry a green or yellow soft fruit
gooseberries, gooseberry bush
gorge a narrow opening between mountains
gorilla the largest kind of ape (See page 11)
gospel the teachings of Jesus Christ

gossip to chatter about people
gossiper, gossiping
govern to rule or manage
governess, government, governor
gown a woman's dress, usually long
grab to catch hold suddenly; to snatch
grabbed, grabbing, grabber
graceful with beautiful movement
gracefully, gracefulness
gradual happening little by little
gradually, gradualness
grain a tiny piece of anything like sand or a seed of corn
gram a unit of weight
grammar the rules for using words
grammatical, ungrammatical
granary a building for storing grain
grand large and important
grandly, grandness, grandstand
grandchild the child of your daughter or son
grandson, grand-daughter, grand-children
grandfather the father of your mother or father
grandad, grandpa
grandmother the mother of your mother or father
grandma, granny
grandparent your grandfather or grandmother
granite a very hard rock

grape black or green fruit grown on a vine and used for making wine

grapefruit a fruit like a large yellow orange

grasp to hold firmly; to seize

grass a plant with thin green leaves growing in fields and on lawns
grass-snake, grasshopper, grassy

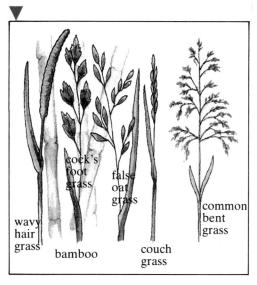

cock's foot grass
false oat grass
common bent grass
wavy hair grass
bamboo
couch grass

grate 1. to cut into tiny bits (grated cheese)
2. a metal frame for holding fuel

grateful thankful; full of thanks
gratefully, gratitude

grave 1. serious
2. a hole dug to bury a dead body
gravestone, graveyard

gravel a mixture of small pebbles used for making paths

gravity the pull of the earth

gravy a sauce made from the juice of cooked meat

graze 1. to feed on grass
2. to scrape something such as your skin
grazing, grazer

grease thick oil or fat
greasy, greasiness

great 1. large
2. important (a great king)
greatly, greatness

greed a desire for more than is necessary
greedy, greedily, greediness

green the colour of growing grass
greengrocer, greenhouse, greenish

greet to welcome someone
greetings

grey the colour between black and white
greyhound, greyness

grew the past tense of 'to grow'

grief deep sorrow or sadness
grieve, grieving, grievance

grim stern; unfriendly
grimly, grimness, grimmer, grimmest

grin to give a big smile
grinned, grinning, grinner

grind to crush into powder (ground coffee)
grinder, grindstone, ground

grip to hold tightly
gripped, gripping

grit tiny pieces of stone
gritty, grittiness, gritted

groan to make a deep sound of pain

grocer someone who sells food such as tea, sugar, butter, and bacon
grocery, groceries

groom someone who looks after horses

groove a narrow cut in something

ground 1. the earth we walk on
  2. the past tense of 'to grind'
group a number of people or things all together
grow 1. to become bigger
  2. to raise plants
  grew, grown, growth
growl to make an angry noise like a dog
grub an insect when it has just hatched
grumble to complain; to find fault
  grumbler, grumbling
grunt to make a noise like a pig
guard 1. to look after or keep safe
  2. the person who is on guard
  guardian, guardsman
guess to try to give the right answer without having real knowledge
  guesses, guesswork
guest someone visiting someone else's house
  guest-house
guide to show the way
  guiding, guidance
guilty having done something wrong
  guilt, guiltily, guiltless
guinea-pig a small pet animal with no tail
guitar a stringed musical instrument
  guitarist

guitar

electric guitar

gulf a large bay; a wide gap
gum 1. the pink flesh round your teeth
  2. a kind of glue
  3. the eucalyptus tree (See page 145)
  gummy, gumminess, gummed
gun any weapon that fires bullets or missiles
  gunboat, gunfire, gunman, gunner, gunnery, gunpowder, gunshot

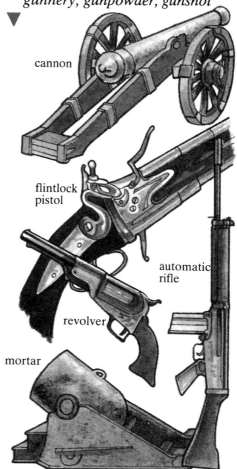

cannon

flintlock pistol

revolver

mortar

automatic rifle

gutter a channel to carry away rain water
gymkhana a display of pony or horse-riding
gymnasium a building for practising physical exercises
  gym, gymnast, gymnastics

Hh

habit something done so often that you do it without thinking
habitual, habitually

haddock a large sea fish

hag an ugly old woman; a witch

hail frozen drops of rain
hailstone, hailstorm

hair the soft threads that grow on the heads and bodies of mammals
hairbrush, haircut, hairdresser, hairless, hairpin, hair-slide, hairy, hairraising

hake a large sea fish

half one of the two equal parts of a whole
half-hearted, half-time, half-way, half-wit, half-witted, halves

hall 1. a large room for meetings
2. the space just inside the front door

halt to stop

halter a rope for leading horses

halve to divide into two equal parts

ham meat from the leg of a pig

hamburger a round piece of fried chopped meat

hammer a tool for hitting nails (See page 141)

hammock a hanging bed, often used in ships

hamster a small pet animal

hand the part of the body at the end of the arm
handbag, handcuffs, handful, handiwork, handrail, handwriting, handy

handicap something that hinders you from doing something else
handicapped, handicapping

handicraft skilful work done with the hands

handkerchief a cloth for wiping your nose

handle the part by which something is held
handlebars, handleless

handsome good-looking
handsomely, handsomeness

hang to fix something at the top so that it is free at the bottom

hangar a large shed for aircraft

happen to take place
happening, happened

happy pleased; full of joy
happily, happiness, happier

harbour a place where ships can shelter and unload

hard 1. not soft
2. difficult; not easy
harden, hardship, hardware, hardy

hardly only just (I can hardly lift it.)

hare a fast animal, like a big rabbit

hark listen (Hark! Was that the bell?)
harm to hurt; to damage
harmful, harmfully, harmless,
harmlessly
harness straps and fittings worn by a
horse
harpoon a spear used in hunting large
fish and whales

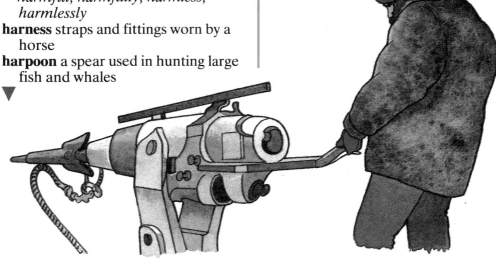

harvest the gathering of food crops
haste hurry
hasten, hastily, hastiness, hasty
hat a covering for the head
hatch 1. to be born by breaking out of
an egg
2. an opening in the deck of a ship
hate to dislike very much
hateful, hating, hatred
haul 1. to pull
2. what you pull in
have to own; to hold
had, has, hasn't, haven't, having
havoc great destruction
hawk a bird of prey

hawthorn a small tree with red berries
hay dried grass for feeding animals
hay-fever, hay-making, hay-stack
hazel a nut tree

hazel
catkins

hazel
nuts

head the part of the body above the
neck
headache, header, heading, head-
light, headline, headlong, head-
master, head-phones, headquarters,
headway, headteacher
heal to make or become well again
health how well or ill a person is
healthy, healthier, healthiest,
healthily, healthiness

heap a pile of things

hear to take in the sounds of things
heard, hearing-aid, hearsay

heart the part of the body that pumps blood round it
heartbeat, heart-breaking, heartbroken, heartily, heartless, hearty, heartiness

hearth the floor of a fire-place

heat warmth
heat-wave, heater

heathen someone who does not believe in God

heather a small plant that grows on moors

heavens the sky

heavy of great weight
heavier, heaviest, heavily, heaviness

hedge a kind of fence made of bushes
hedgerow, hedging

hedgehog a small animal covered in prickles

heel 1. the back part of the foot
2. the back part of a boot or shoe

heifer a young cow

height the distance from top to bottom

heir someone who receives the belongings of a dead person
heiress, heirloom

helicopter an aircraft with rotors instead of wings

helm the tiller or wheel used to steer a ship or boat
helmsman

helmet a covering to protect the head

help to make it easier for someone by sharing the work
helpful, helpfully, helpless, helplessly

hem the edge of a piece of cloth where it has been turned over and stitched
hem-line, hemmed, hemming

hen 1. any female bird
2. a female chicken

herd a large group of cattle

here in this place

hermit someone who lives alone in a lonely place

hero a very brave person
heroes, heroic, heroically, heroine, heroism

heron a long-legged bird (See page 20)

herring a sea fish that is often kippered

herself (She has cut herself.)

hesitate to pause uncertainly
hesitant, hesitantly, hesitation

hexagon a flat shape with six sides

hide to put out of sight
hide-and-seek, hiding-place, hide-out, hidden, hide-away

high 1. going up a long way
2. the measurement from top to bottom
highbrow, highlands, highlight, highly, highway, highwayman

hill a place where the ground is higher than the rest
hillside, hilltop, hilly

himself (Tom has hurt himself.)

hinder to delay by getting in the way
hindrance

Hindu a believer in Hinduism, an Indian religion

hinge a device on which a door swings

hint to suggest

hip 1. the bony part of the body just above your legs
2. the fruit of the wild rose

hippopotamus a large land and river animal
hippopotamuses

hire to borrow something for money
hiring, hire-purchase

hiss to make a noise like an 's'

history the study of times past
historic, historical, historian

hit to strike; to bump into
hitting

hive a place where bees live

hoard to collect and store things

hoarse rough (a hoarse voice)

hobby something you like doing in your spare time
hobbies

hockey a team game played with special sticks

hoe a tool used for weeding and digging (See page 141)

hold 1. to have something in the hand
2. to contain (This bottle holds a litre.)
3. the part of the ship that holds the cargo
held, holdall, holder, hold-up

hole an opening; a hollow

holiday a day or period of time when there is no work

hollow having a space inside; empty

holly an evergreen tree with prickly leaves (See page 144)

holy sacred; belonging to God

home the place where you live
home-made, homeless, homely, homesick, homeward, homework, homing pigeon

honest not lying or cheating; trustworthy
honestly, honesty

honey a sweet food made by bees
honeycomb, honeymoon, honeysuckle

honour great respect
honourable, honourably

hood 1. a covering for the neck and head
2. a cover for a pram or open car
3. the bonnet of a car in American English

hoof the hard part of the foot of a horse, cow, pig, etc.
hoofs or *hooves*

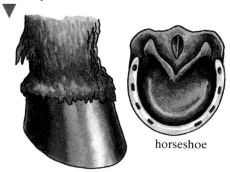

horseshoe

hook a bent piece of metal for hanging things on, or catching fish

hoop a large ring
hoop-la

hoot to make the noise of a car horn

hop to jump around on one foot
hopped, hopping, hopper

hope to want something to happen
hopeful, hopefully, hopeless, hope-lessly, hopelessness, hoping

horizon the line where sky and earth seem to meet

horn 1. the hard spike on some animals' heads
2. a devise for making warning sounds
3. a musical instrument (See page 90)

cow

wild goat

rhinoceros

horrid very nasty

horror a feeling of great fear
horrible, horribly, horrific

horse an animal used for riding
horseback, horse-box, horseman, horsemanship, horse-power, horse-shoe, horsewoman

hospital a place where sick people are taken care of

hot not cold, very warm
hot-house, hot-pot, hotter, hottest

hotel a building where people pay to stay

hour a length of time: 60 minutes
hourly, hour-glass

house a building to live in
house-boat, household, house-keeper, house-proud, housewife, housework

hover to hang still in the air like a bird
hovercraft, hoverfly

howl a long loud cry

hug to hold lovingly in the arms
hugged, hugging

huge very large

hull the body of a ship

hum to make a murmuring sound
hummed, humming, humming bird

human like or belonging to mankind
human being, humanity

humble simple and in no way costly; modest
humbling, humbly, humbleness

humour being funny; a sense of fun
humorous, humorously, humorist

hump a big bump (a camel's hump)

hundred the number 100

hundredth, hundredweight
hungry feeling in need of food
hungrily, hunger
hunt 1. to try to catch wild animals
2. to look carefully for something
hunter, huntsman
hurricane a very violent windy storm
hurry to want to get something done
quickly
hurried, hurriedly, hurries, hurrying
hurt to make someone feel pain
husband a married man
hut a small building used as a shelter
hutch a box for a pet rabbit to live in

hovercraft

hyacinth a garden flower, usually blue
in colour
hyena an animal with a cry like a laugh
hymn a religious song of praise
hyphen the mark (-) to divide a word

Ii

ice frozen water
*iceberg, icecream, icicle, icy,
icebreaker, ice-hockey*
idea a thought; a plan
ideal 1. perfect
2. something to live up to
ideally, idealistic, idealism
idiot a very stupid person
idiotic, idiotically, idiocy
idle not working, lazy
idleness, idling, idly
igloo an Eskimo's house made of
blocks of ice or snow
ignorant knowing little or nothing
*ignorance, ignorantly, ignore,
ignoring*
ill not well; in bad health
*ill-mannered, ill-tempered,
ill-treatment*
illustrate to explain with the help of
pictures
illustrated, illustration
imagine to form pictures in the mind
*imaginable, imaginary, imagina-
tion, imaginative, imaginatively*
imitate to do the same as someone
else; to copy
imitation, imitator, imitating
immediate happening at once
immediately
immense very big
immensely
immigrant someone coming to settle
in your country
immigrate, immigration
immortal living for ever
impartial very fair
impatient not willing to wait
impatience, impatiently
imperfect not perfect; damaged
impertinent not respectful, rude

impolite rude; not polite

import to bring goods into your country

important needing to be treated seriously
importance, importantly

impossible not able to be done
impossibility, impossibly

imprison to put into prison

improve to make or get better
improvement, improving

inch a measure of length; 2.5cm

include to put something with the others
including, inclusion, inclusive

income money received

incorrect wrong; not correct

increase to make or become greater

independent not controlled by anyone else
independence, independently

index an alphabetical list showing the contents of a book
indexes, index finger

indicate to point something out
indicator, indication, indicative

indoors inside a building

infant a very young child
infancy

influenza a fever often called 'flu'

inform to tell someone something
informer, information, informative

inhabit to live in
inhabitable, inhabitant

initials the first letters of a person's names

injection to put medicine into your body through a needle

injure to hurt or damage
injury, injuries

ink coloured liquid for writing

inland away from the coast

inn a small hotel; a public house

innings the time during which a player or team is batting in cricket

innocent having done nothing wrong
innocence, innocently

inquire to ask for information
inquiring, inquiry

insane mad
insanely, insanity

insect a small animal with six legs

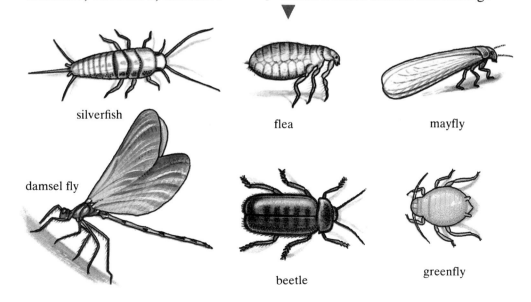

silverfish

flea

mayfly

damsel fly

beetle

greenfly

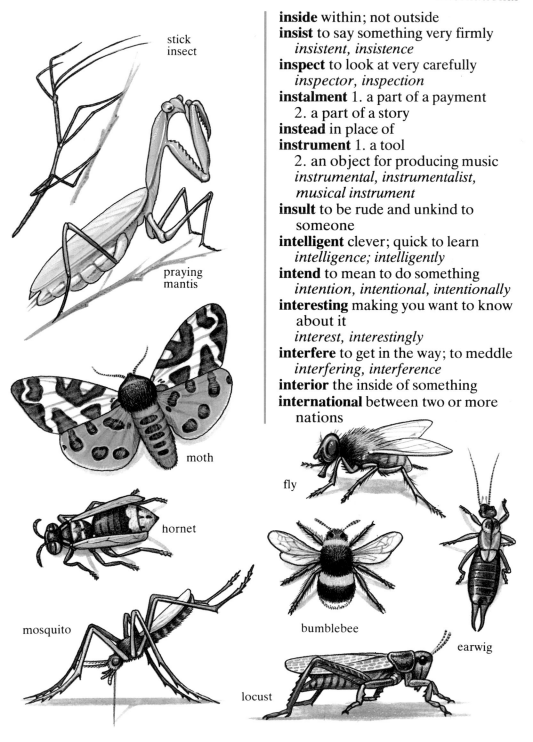

stick insect

praying mantis

moth

hornet

mosquito

fly

bumblebee

earwig

locust

inside within; not outside
insist to say something very firmly
insistent, insistence
inspect to look at very carefully
inspector, inspection
instalment 1. a part of a payment
2. a part of a story
instead in place of
instrument 1. a tool
2. an object for producing music
instrumental, instrumentalist,
musical instrument
insult to be rude and unkind to
someone
intelligent clever; quick to learn
intelligence; intelligently
intend to mean to do something
intention, intentional, intentionally
interesting making you want to know
about it
interest, interestingly
interfere to get in the way; to meddle
interfering, interference
interior the inside of something
international between two or more
nations

interrupt to break in and stop something
interruption

interval a break between two parts of a play

introduce 1. to bring something into use
2. to make two people known to each other
introducing, introduction, introductory

invade to enter a country by force
invader, invading, invasion

invalid someone who is ill a long time

invent 1. to make something up
2. to make something that has not been made before
invention, inventive, invention

invisible not able to be seen
invisibility, invisibly

invite to ask someone to come
inviting, invitation, invitingly

iris 1. the coloured part of the eyeball
2. a garden flower

iron 1. a strong hard metal
2. a device for smoothing clothes
ironmonger, electric iron

irrigate to supply dry land with water
irrigating, irrigation

irritate 1. to annoy
2. to cause an itch
irritating, irritation, irritable

island a piece of land surrounded by water

itch to have a tickling feeling

item one thing from a list

itself (The cat is scratching itself.)

ivory the hard material of an elephant's tusk

ivy a climbing evergreen plant

Jj

jacaranda a tree with colourful flowers (See page 145)

jack a tool for lifting

jackal a wild animal of the dog family

jackdaw a black bird (See page 20)

jacket a short coat

jagged with rough edges

jaguar a wild animal of the cat family

jail a prison

jam 1. fruit boiled with sugar
2. to squeeze; to become stuck tight
jammed, jamming

January the first month of the year

jar a container made of glass or pottery

jaw the bone of your mouth from which the teeth grow

jazz a kind of music first played by blacks in the USA

jealous wanting what someone else has
jealously, jealousy

jeans close-fitting trousers

jeep a kind of car for driving over rough ground

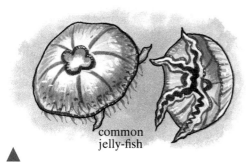
common
jelly-fish

▲

jelly a wobbly food that melts
jellied, jelly-fish, jellies
jerk to make a sudden pull or push
jersey a knitted covering for the top
part of your body
jet liquid or gas forced out of a small
opening to power an engine
jet engine, jet plane
Jew a believer in the Hebrew religion
Jewish
jewel any precious stone
jeweller, jewellery
jigsaw a picture made by fitting pieces
together
job work you are paid to do; a task
jockey a rider of race-horses
jodhpurs special trousers for riding
jog 1. to run along at a steady pace
2. to knock something slightly
jogged, jogging, jogger, jogtrot
join 1. to fix together
2. to become a member of a group
joiner, joinery, joint
joke something said to make you laugh
jolly merry; happy
journalist a person who writes for a
newspaper
journey a distance travelled
joy a feeling of great happiness
joyful, joyfully, joyous
judge 1. someone who decides who is
right in a court of law
2. to decide who or which is best
judging, judgement
jug a container with a handle and lip

juggler someone who does tricks such
as balancing things or keeping them
in the air
juggle, juggling
juice the liquid from fruit, meat or
vegetables
juicy
July the seventh month of the year
jumble 1. a muddle
2. unwanted clothes
jumbo very large (a jumbo jet)
jump to spring into the air with both
feet
jumper 1. someone who jumps
2. a jersey
junction a place where two lines meet
June the sixth month of the year
jungle thick forest in a hot country
junior younger
junk 1. rubbish
2. a Chinese sailing-boat

▼

just 1. fair
2. exactly (just right)
3. a moment ago (He has just left.)
justly, justice

Kk

kangaroo a jumping Australian animal
karate a Japanese form of self-defence
kayak an Eskimo canoe
keel the long strip of wood or metal at the bottom of a boat
keen 1. very interested in doing something
2. sharp like a knife's blade
keenly, keenness
keep 1. to hold on to something for yourself
2. the strongest part of a castle
keeper, kept, keep-sake
kennel a hut in which a dog can live
kerb the edge of the pavement
kerbstone
kernel the central and eatable part of a nut
kettle a metal container with a spout for boiling water

key 1. a device for locking and unlocking
2. a part to be pressed on a piano or a typewriter
keyboard, keyhole
kick to hit with your foot
kicker, kick-off
kid 1. a young goat
2. a child (slang)
kidnap to take someone away by force
kidnapper, kidnapping, kidnapped
kill to take life away
kilogram a measure of weight; 1,000 grams
kilometre a measure of distance; 1,000 metres
kilt a kind of skirt worn by men in Scotland
kind 1. good to other people; helpful
2. a sort or type of thing
kindness, kind-hearted, kindly

Inside a castle keep

king the crowned male ruler of a country
kingdom, kingly
kingfisher a colourful river bird

kiosk 1. a public telephone box
2. a small covered stall
kipper a smoked herring
kiss to touch someone with your lips
kit the things needed for doing something
kitchen a room where food is cooked
kite 1. a toy that flies
2. a meat-eating bird
kitten a young cat
kiwi a New Zealand bird

knee the joint where your leg bends
kneel to go down on your knees
knelt
knickers a garment worn by girls; pants
knife a tool with a sharp blade
knives, knifed, knifing
knight 1. a man with the title 'Sir'
2. in the Middle Ages a gentleman who fought on horseback for the king
knighthood
knit to weave with long needles
knitted, knitting-needles
knob a round handle; a lump
knobbly
knock to hit or bump into
knocker, knock-kneed, knock-out
knot 1. the place where string is tied
2. a measure of speed for ships
knotted, knotting, knotty
know 1. to be sure about something
2. to be able to recognize someone
know-all, know-how, knowing, knowingly
knowledge your understanding of everything
knowledgeable, knowledgeably
knuckle a joint in a finger
koala a small furry Australian animal

kookaburra an Australian bird with a cry like a laugh (See page 20)
Koran the holy book of Islam

Ll

label a piece of paper or card attached to something saying what it is
labelled, labelling

laboratory a place for scientific experiments

labour heavy work
laborious, laboriously, labourer

lace 1. pretty material like a net
2. something to tie up a shoe
lacing, laced, lacy

lack to be without something you need

lad a boy

ladder wooden or metal steps for climbing

ladle a deep spoon with a long handle

lady a polite word for a woman
ladies, lady-like

ladybird a flying beetle with spots (See page 18)

lagoon a shallow salt-water lake

laid from 'to lay' (The hen has laid an egg.)

lain from 'to lie' (He has lain there a long time.)

lake an area of water surrounded by land

lamb a young sheep

lame not able to walk properly

lamp a light usually covered with glass
lamp-post, lamp-shade

land 1. the part of the earth not covered with sea
2. a piece of ground
3. to come onto land from the sea or the air
landing-stage, landing-strip, landmark, landscape, landslide

landlady (landlord) a woman (or man) who lets land or a house for rent
landladies

lane a narrow country road

language the words used in speech or writing

lantern a box with windows to hold a light

larch a coniferous tree

large big
largeness, largely

lark a small singing bird (See page 21)

larva the grub or caterpillar form of an insect

lass a girl
lasses

lasso a looped rope to catch animals

last 1. coming after all the others
2. to go on for some time
3. a shape used for making and repairing shoes

late after the right time

latter the second of two things just mentioned

laugh the sound you make when amused
laughable, laughter, laughing-stock

rocket

gantry

launching pad

launch 1. a powerful motor boat
2. to slide a ship into the water
launching pad
laundry 1. clothes that are being washed
2. a place where clothes are washed
lavatory a water-closet; a loo or toilet
lavatories
law a rule made by the government
lawcourt, lawful, lawyer, lawless
lawn a well-kept patch of grass
lawn-mower
lawyer a person who has studied law
lay 1. to put down carefully
2. to produce eggs
3. the past tense of 'lie' (We lay down in the hay and went to sleep.)
laid, lay-by, layer

lazy not wanting to work
lazier, laziest, lazily, laziness
lead – rhyming with 'fed' – 1. a heavy metal
2. the part of the pencil that makes marks
lead – rhyming with 'feed' – to go first and show the way
2. strip of leather or chain for leading dog
leader, leadership, led
leaf a flat green part of a plant
leafless, leaflet, leafy, leaves
leak a hole that lets gas or liquid escape
leaky, leakiness
lean 1. having no fat
2. thin
3. to hold yourself up against something; to bend towards something
leant, lean-to
leap to jump
leaped, leapt, leap-frog, leap-year
learn to get to know something by working at it
learned, learnt
least the smallest
leather material made from animal skins
leave 1. to go away from
2. to put something down and let it stay
leaving, left
lecture a talk by an expert
lecturer, lecturing
ledge a shelf
leek an onion-like vegetable
left the opposite side to the right
leg a part of the body used for walking
legend an old story handed down from the past
legendary
leisure spare time
lemon a yellow fruit with acid juice
(See page 59)

lemonade, lemon squeezer

lend to give something to someone for a time, after which they give it back

length the distance from end to end
lengthen, lengthy, lengthily

lens curved glass for focusing in cameras, spectacles, microscopes etc

leopard a spotted wild animal of the cat family

less not as much; a smaller amount

lesson something that you can learn

let 1. to allow something to happen
2. to allow someone to use your house for rent
letting

letter 1. one of the parts of the alphabet
2. a message sent by post
letter-box, lettering

lettuce a green vegetable used in salads

level flat and even; the same height
levelled, levelling, levelcrossing, level-headed

lever 1. a tool that helps to lift or move things (a tyre lever)
2. a handle to a machine (a gear lever)

liar someone who tells a lie

liberty freedom

library a place where books are kept
librarian, libraries

lice the plural of louse

licence a printed paper proving you are allowed to do something, such as drive a car

lick to touch something with your tongue

lid a cover for a container
lidded, lidless

lie 1. to rest in a flat position
2. to say something you know to be untrue

life the time that you are alive
lifeboat, life-guard, life-jacket,

lifeless, lifelike, lifelong, lives

lift 1. to move higher
2. a kind of cage that goes up and down from one floor to another

light 1. something which shines brightly
2. not heavy; easy to lift
3. to set on fire
lighten, lighter, lighthouse, lightness, light-hearted, lightship

lightning flashes during a thunderstorm

like 1. the same as; similar to
2. to be fond of
likeable, likeness, likewise

likely to be expected; probable
likelihood

lilac a flowering bush

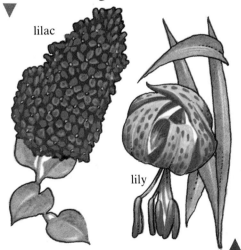

lilac

lily

lily a flower that grows from a bulb

limb an arm or a leg

lime 1. a white powder used in building
2. a fruit with acid juice; the tree on which the fruit grows
3. a tree with small yellow flowers
lime-juice, limelight, limestone

limit the end of something

limp 1. to walk with a bad leg
2. hanging loosely, not stiff

limpet a small clinging shellfish

line 1. a long narrow mark (You draw a
line.)
2. a length of string or wire
3. a row (a line of children)
linen 1. cloth woven from flax
2. things such as sheets, towels,
tablecloths
liner a large passenger ship
link one ring in a chain

lion a wild animal of the cat family
lip one of the edges of the mouth
liquid something that can be poured
list things written down one under the
other
listen to try to hear something
literature stories, plays, poems, etc.
litre a measure of liquids; about 1¾
pints
litter 1. rubbish left lying about
2. a family of animals born together
little small; not much
live 1. to be alive
2. to make one's home somewhere
liver part of the inside of your body
lizard a reptile with four legs

llama a South American animal
load something to be carried
loaf bread baked in a special shape
loaves
loan something which is lent
loathe to hate
loathing, loathsome
lobster a shellfish with two large claws
(See page 119)
local belonging to the area nearby
locality, locally
loch a Scottish lake
lock 1. to shut with a key
2. a place on a canal where the level
of the water can be changed
3. a tress of hair

locomotive a railway engine
locust an insect like a grasshopper (See page 72)
loft a room just under the roof
log 1. a piece of wood cut off a tree trunk
2. a ship's diary
loiter to hang about doing nothing
lollipop a sweet on a stick
lolly, lollies
lonely sad because alone
loneliness
long far from one end to the other
loo a short word for a lavatory
look to turn the eyes to something
loom a machine for weaving cloth
loose free to move; not tight
loosely, looseness, loosen
lorry a motor vehicle for carrying heavy loads
lorries
lose 1. to put something where you cannot find it
2. to be beaten in a game
loser, losing, loss, lost
loud noisy; able to be heard easily
loud-speaker, loudly, loudness

lounge 1. a sitting-room
2. to sit about in a lazy way
lounger, lounging
louse an insect pest
love to like very much
lovable, lover, loving
lovely beautiful; nice to look at
low 1. not high; near the ground
2. to make a sound like a cow
loyal faithful and true
loyally, loyalty
luck something good or bad that happens by chance
lucky, luckier, luckiest, luckily
luggage any container for clothes and other things needed when travelling; baggage
lumberjack a person who cuts down trees
lump 1. a piece without much shape
2. a bump or swelling
lumpy, lumpiness
lunar belonging to the moon
lunatic someone who is mad
lunch a meal in the middle of the day
lungs the part of the body used for breathing

Mm

machine a device that makes things, or does work
machine-gun, machinery

mackerel a sea fish

mackintosh a coat that keeps the rain out

mad ill in your mind; crazy
madden, madder, maddest, madman

magazine a thin book published regularly

magic the pretended art of controlling nature
magical, magically, magician

magnet a piece of metal that attracts or pulls pieces of iron
magnetic, magnetism, magnetize

magnificent grand; splendid to look at
magnificence, magnificently

magnify to make larger
magnified, magnifies, magnification

magpie a large bird (See page 20)

maid a female servant

mail letters or parcels sent by post

main the most important; chief
mainland, mainly

maize a kind of cereal; (See page 29)

majesty a title for a king or queen
majestic, majestically

major 1. of great importance (a major event)
2. an army office above a captain
majority, majorities

make 1. to build; bring into being
2. to cause or force (He made me do it.)
made, making, make-up, makeshift

malaria an illness caused by mosquitoes

male a man or a boy

mammal any animal that feeds its young with its own milk

mammoth a large extinct kind of elephant

man a grown-up male person
manhood, manly, men

manage 1. to be in charge of (The person who manages the office is the manager.)
2. to be able to (We at last managed to open the door.)
manageable, management, managing, manager

mane the long hair on the neck of an animal, especially a horse

manger an open feeding box for cows or horses

manner the way something is done

manufacture to make things by machine
manufacturer, manufacturing

many a lot of

map a drawing showing the shape of a country, sea, town, etc

maple a tree (See page 145)

marble a small glass ball used as a toy

March the third month of the year

march to walk like soldiers

mare a female horse

margarine a food used instead of butter

margin the space down the side of a piece of writing

mariner a sailor

mark 1. a spot or stain
2. a number to show how good your work is

market a place where things are bought and sold in the open
market-day, market-place

marmalade jam made from oranges

marriage 1. when a man and a woman are husband and wife
2. a wedding

marry to become husband and wife
married, marries, marrying

marsh soft wet ground
marshes, marshy

marsupial a mammal with a pouch

martyr someone who dies for what he believes

marvellous wonderful
marvel, marvelled, marvellously

mascot something that is supposed to bring good luck

masculine belonging to men

mask a disguise for the face

mason a person who builds with stone

mass a large quantity

mast a pole used to hold up sails or flags

master the man in charge; a male teacher

mat 1. a small rug
2. something put under hot dishes

match 1. a tiny stick for lighting things
2. a game between two teams
3. to sort by size, colour, shape
matches, matchable, matching

mate 1. someone you work or play with
2. one of the officers on a ship
3. to come together to have young ones

material any substance for making things

mathematics the study of numbers and measurements
maths, mathematical

matron the woman in charge of the nurses in a hospital

matter 1. anything that can be seen and touched
2. to be important (Keeping fit matters a lot to everyone.)
3. something to be thought about (I will think about the matter and let you know.)

mattress the soft part of the bed you sleep on

mauve a pale colour made by mixing red and blue; purple

May the fifth month of the year

mayor/mayoress the man or woman chosen as the leader of a town

meadow a field of grass

meal breakfast, lunch, tea, dinner or supper

mean 1. selfish
2. to show or indicate
3. to intend or plan (I meant to do it.)
meaning, meaningless, meant, meanness

measles an illness with red spots

measure to find the size or amount
measurable, measurement, measuring

meat the flesh of an animal used for food

mechanic a person who repairs machines

Victoria Cross

Distinguished Service Order

Military Cross

General Service Medal

South Atlantic Medal

French Military Medal 1852–70

1914–18 War Medal

1919 Victory Medal

American Purple Heart

medal a piece of metal like a coin given as a reward

medicine a pill or liquid taken to make an ill person better
medical, medically

meet to come together

melody a tune
melodies, melodious

melon a large juicy fruit (See page 59)

melt to change into liquid by using heat

member someone who belongs to a group
membership

memory the ability to remember
memorable, memorably, memorial, memories, memorize, memorizing

mend to put right

mental to do with the mind
mentality, mentally

mention to speak about something

merchant someone who buys and sells goods

mercury a silvery liquid metal

mercy not using one's power to hurt
mercies, merciful, mercifully, merciless, mercilessly

mere no more than (He is a mere child.)
merely

mermaid a make-believe creature half woman, half fish

merry happy; very cheerful
merrier, merriest, merrily,
merriment, merry-go-round

mess a dirty or untidy state of things
messy, messily, messiness

message a piece of information from
one person to another
messenger

metal a hard material such as iron,
gold, copper, silver
metallic

meteor a shooting star

meter an instrument for measuring
a gas meter, a parking meter

method the way in which something is
done
methodical, methodically

metre a measurement of length; 100
centimetres

mice the plural of mouse

microphone an instrument for picking
up sound waves

microscope an instrument that makes
tiny things look much bigger
microscopic

midday 12 o'clock in the middle of the
day; noon

middle the point which is the same
distance from each side

midnight 12 o'clock at night

might 1. to be possible (I think he
might help us.)
2. great strength or power
mighty, mightily

mild gentle; not extreme
mildly, mildness

mile a measure of distance; 1.61
kilometres
mileage, milestone

military to do with soldiers

milk the white liquid that female
animals such as cows produce to
feed their young
milkman, milky, milking-machine

mill 1. a factory making cloth or steel

2. a place where corn is ground into
flour
miller, pepper-mill

milligram a measure of weight

millimetre a measure of length

million a thousand thousands;
1,000,000

millionaire a very rich person

mince to chop meat into tiny pieces
mincemeat, mincer, mincing

mind 1. the thinking part of the brain
2. to look after (Mind my clothes,
please.)
3. not to really want to do something
(Do you mind stopping?)
minder, mindless, baby-minding

mine 1. belonging to me
2. a deep hole for digging coal, iron,
etc.
miner, mining

mineral 1. material dug from the earth
such as coal, rock, iron
2. a semi-precious stone

▼

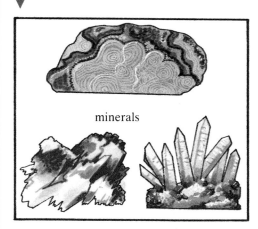

minerals

mini small
mini-bus, mini-skirt

minimum smallest; least

minister 1. someone who takes
services in a church
2. an important member of the
government

minor not very important

mint 1. a green plant with a strong taste
2. a place where coins are made

minus less; the sign – (Ten minus six equals four; $10 - 6 = 4$)

minute a measure of time; 60 seconds

minute very small (pronounced my-newt)

miracle a wonderful and surprising happening
miraculous, miraculously

mirror a glass in which you can see yourself

mirth laughter; joy

mischief silly things done to annoy
mischievous, mischievously

miser someone who does not like spending money even when he has a lot
miserly, miserliness

miserable very unhappy
miserably, misery

mislead to lead the wrong way; to deceive

miss 1. a word used in front of an unmarried female's name (Miss Jones)
2. to fail to hit, reach, catch, etc.
3. to realise that something has gone

missile a weapon or object thrown

mist a thin cloud near the ground
misty, mistiness

mistake something done wrongly
mistaken, mistakenly, mistook

mistletoe a plant with white berries that grows on trees

mistress the woman in charge

misunderstand to understand wrongly
misunderstood

mix to shake or stir things up together
mixes, mixture

moan to make a sound as if in pain

moat a wide ditch with water round a castle

mob a noisy and dangerous crowd
mobbed, mobbing

mock to make fun of
mockery

model 1. a small but good copy of something
2. a person who shows off clothes
modelled, modelling

moderate not too much and not too little
moderately, moderation

modern up-to-date; not old-fashioned
modernize, modernization

modest not praising yourself too much
modestly, modesty

module part of a space vehicle

moist slightly wet; damp
moisten, moisture

mole 1. a small underground animal
2. a dark spot on your skin

molecule a small group of atoms; a particle

moment a very short time

monastery a place where monks live and work
monasteries, monastic

Monday the second day of the week

money coins and notes used to buy things

mongrel a dog that is a mixture of two or more kinds

monk a religious man who lives with other monks in a monastery

howler monkey

mandrill

baboon

rhesus monkey

▲

monkey a climbing wild animal

monster a frightening animal in fairy stories
monstrous, monstrously, monstrosity

month one of the twelve parts of a year

monument a building to remind you of an important happening

mood the state your mind is in
moody, moodily, moodiness

moon the heavenly body that circles the earth
moonbeam, moonlight, moonless

moor 1. rough ground where little grows
2. to fasten a boat to stop it drifting
mooring, moorland, moorhen

moose a large wild animal like a deer

mop material at the end of a stick for wiping floors
mopped, mopping

more greater; a greater quantity
moreover

morning the part of the day before midday

Moslem a follower of Mohammed; a believer in the religion of Islam

mosque a building where Moslems worship

mosquito a small biting insect (See page 73)
mosquitoes

moss a plant that grows on trees and stones

most the largest quantity; nearly all

moth an insect like a butterfly that usually flies at night
moth-ball, moth-eaten

▼

hawk moth

mother a woman who has children

motion movement

motor an engine that makes things move
motor boat, motor bike, motor car, motor cycle, motorist, motorway

motto a short saying to help you lead a good life

moult to lose fur, feathers or hair

mountain a large and high hill
mountaineer, mountainous

mourn to be sad because someone is dead
mourner, mournful

mouse a small animal with a long tail
mice, mousetrap

▼

moustache the hair that grows between the nose and mouth of a man

mouth the opening in your face for eating and talking
mouth-organ, mouthful

move 1. to put in another place
2. to go to another place
movable, movement, moving

mow to cut grass
mower, mown

Mr the polite word before a man's name (Mr James Smith)

Mrs the polite word before a married woman's name (Mrs Julia Smith)

much 1. a large amount
2. greatly (They enjoyed their holiday very much.)

mud very wet earth
mudguard, muddy, muddied

muddle a mix up
muddling

mug a large cup without a saucer

multiply to make a number greater (Three multiplied by four equals twelve.)
multiplication, multiplies, multiplying

multitude a huge crowd

mum a short way of saying mother
mummy, mummies

mumble to speak very unclearly
mumbler, mumbling

mumps an illness which gives you a swollen neck

murder the crime of deliberately killing someone
murderer, murderous

murmur a soft low sound

muscle a part of the body that helps you move
muscular

museum a building where interesting old things are put on show

mushroom a small plant often shaped like an umbrella; a fungus

▼

parasol mushroom

button mushrooms

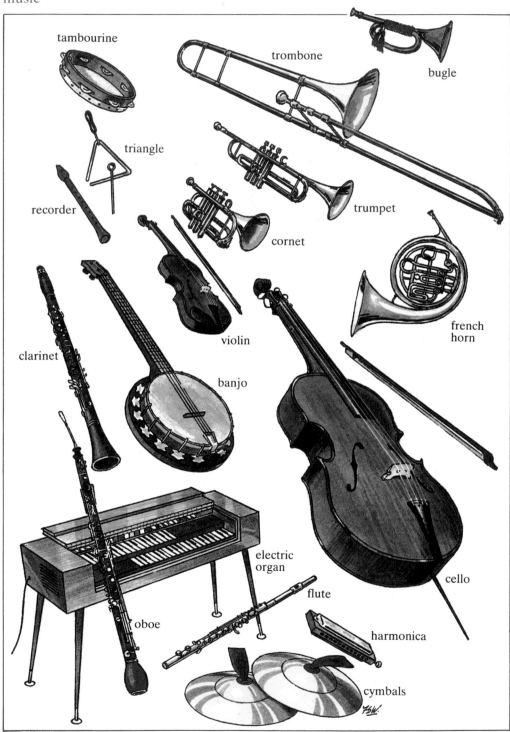

tambourine

trombone

bugle

triangle

recorder

trumpet

cornet

french horn

clarinet

violin

banjo

electric organ

cello

flute

oboe

harmonica

cymbals

music pleasant sounds made by singing or playing musical instruments
musical, musician

mussel a shellfish

must to have to

mustard a hot yellow paste to flavour food

mutiny an open rebellion by sailors
mutineer, mutinies, mutinied, mutinous

mutter to speak in a low voice

mutton meat from sheep

muzzle 1. the open end of a gun
2. a covering for the mouth of an animal to stop it biting

myself (I have hurt myself.)

mystery something strange and hard to explain
mysteries, mysterious, mysteriously

Nn

nail 1. a pointed piece of metal for joining two pieces of wood
2. the horny part at the end of a finger or toe
nail-brush, nail-scissors

naked with no clothes on
nakedly, nakedness

name what a thing or person is called
naming, nameless

nappy a piece of material to put round a baby's bottom
nappies, napkin

narrow not measuring much across; not wide

nasty unpleasant; not nice
nastier, nastiest, nastiness, nastily

nation a country and its people
national, nationality, nationalize

native a person born in the country mentioned (He is a native of France.)

natural as nature made it; not artificial
naturally

nature all the things of the world not made by man

naughty badly behaved
naughtily, naughtiness, naughtier

navy the warships and sailors of a country
naval, navies

near close to; not far away
nearly, nearness

neat everything clean and in order; tidy
neatly, neatness

necessary having to be done; needed
necessarily, necessity, necessities

neck the part joining your head to your shoulders
necklace

need not to have something you want; to require
needy, needless

neigh to make a sound like a horse

neighbour a person who lives very near
neighbourhood, neighbourly

neither not one thing or the other

nephew a son of your brother or sister

nerve a thread-like part that carries messages from the brain to other parts of the body

nervous easily frightened
nervously, nervousness, nervy

nest the home a bird makes for itself

weaver bird

reed warbler

martin

net thread woven into a pattern of holes
netting, netted, netball

nettle a wild plant (a stinging nettle)

never not at any time
nevermore, nevertheless

new just made or bought; not old

news information about what has happened
newsagent, newspaper

newt a small lizard-like pond animal

crested newt

next nearest; what follows

nib the writing part of a pen

nibble to eat with quick tiny bites
nibbling, nibbler

nice pleasant

nickname a name people use instead of your proper name

niece the daughter of your brother or sister

night the time between sunset and dawn
nightdress, nightfall, nightly, nightmare, night-watchman

nil nothing; no score

nightingale a small song-bird (See page 20)

nine the number 9
ninth

nineteen the number 19
nineteenth

ninety the number 90
nintieth

nipper a small child

noble 1. of fine character
2. a person of high rank
nobly, nobleman, nobility

nobody no persons; no one

noise a loud sound, often unpleasant
noisy, noisily, noisiness

nomad a member of a wandering tribe

none not any

nonsense words that do not mean anything
nonsensical

noon 12 o'clock in the middle of the day

normal usual; ordinary
normally, normality

north one of the four main compass points
northerly, northern, northward

nose the part of the face you smell with
nosey, nosing, nosily

nostril one of the two openings of the nose

note 1. a musical sound
2. a piece of paper money
3. a short message to yourself or someone else
notebook, notable, noteworthy

nothing not anything

notice 1. to see something
2. a piece of information put up to be read
noticeable, notice-board, noticing

nought the number 0; zero

noun a word used to name something (Tom, room, bravery, London are all nouns.)

novel 1. a book with one long story
2. new and a little strange
novelist, novelty

November the eleventh month of the year

now at this very moment

nuisance anything which annoys

number a word or figure telling you how many
numberless

numerous very many

nun a religious woman who lives with other nuns

nurse a person trained to look after the sick

nursery 1. a place where young children play or sleep
2. a place where young plants are grown
nurseries, nursery rhyme, nursery school

nut 1. a fruit with a hard shell
2. the object that screws on to a bolt
nutcrackers, nutshell

nylon a strong man-made thread

Oo

oak a tree (See page 144)

oar a pole with a flat end to row a boat
oarsman

oasis a place in a desert where there is water
oases

oats a cereal used for making porridge (See page 29)

obey to do as you are told
obedient, obediently, obedience

object 1. something you can see or touch
2. to give reasons for not doing something
objection, objectionable, objector

oblige to do someone a good turn
obliging, obligingly

oblong a shape with two long sides like a book

observe to watch carefully
observant, observer, observing

obstacle something that gets in your way

obtain to get
obtainable

obvious easy to see or understand

occasional happening from time to time

occupation a job

occupy to take up space
occupied, occupies, occupying

occur to happen
occurred, occurring, occurrence

ocean a large sea

o'clock the time by the clock

October the tenth month of the year

octopus a sea animal with eight arms

odd 1. strange (He's an odd boy.)
2. unable to be divided by two (1, 3, 5, 7 are odd numbers.)
oddment, oddity, oddities

off not on
offside

offend to hurt someone's feelings
offender, offensive, offence

offer 1. to say you are ready to do something
2. to hold something out to someone

office a room or building where people work

officer a person who gives orders, especially in the armed forces

often over and over again

oil a greasy liquid used for making petrol
oil-can, oil-field, oil-tanker, oil-well, oily, oiliness, oilskins

ointment a healing paste to put on cuts

old having great age; not new
old-fashioned, olden days

olive a bitter-tasting fruit

omit to leave out
omission, omitted, omitting

once one time

one the number 1
oneself, one-way

onion a vegetable with a bulb

only by itself; no more

open not closed
opening, openness

opera a play where the actors sing instead of speaking

operate 1. to work (How does this machine operate?)
2. to perform a surgical operation
operating, operation, operator

opinion what you think to be true

opportunity a good chance to do something
opportunities

opposite 1. facing; on the other side
2. as different as possible

oral spoken aloud

orange 1. a round juicy fruit (See page 59)
2. the colour of this fruit
orangeade, orange-squash

orbit the path of a planet or other heavenly body through space

orchard a field of fruit trees

orchid a flower

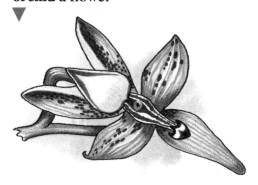

order 1. a command
2. tidiness
3. arrangement (alphabetical order)

ordinary usual; common
ordinarily, ordinariness

ore a rock from which metal can be obtained

organ a musical instrument with pipes and a keyboard

organize to get people to do things
organization, organizer, organizing

original the first one
origin, originally, originality

ornament a decoration for a person or a room
ornamental

orphan a child whose parents are dead

ostrich the largest living bird (See page 20)

other not this one; different

otter an animal living in or near water

ought should; must

ounce a unit of weight; 28.3 grams

our belonging to us
ours

out not in; away
outdoors, outing, outlaw, outline, outside, outsider, outskirts, outstanding

oval shaped like an egg

oven a closed space where food is baked

over 1. above
2. finished

overall, overboard, overcoat,
overflow, overgrown, overhead,
overhear, overseas, oversleep,
overtime, overturn, overtake

owe to have to pay back something
owing

owl a night bird

own 1. to have something that belongs
to you
2. (To own up means to admit.)
owner, ownership

ox one of a family of animals related to
domestic cattle
oxen

oxygen one of the gases in air needed
to breathe

oyster a shellfish that can be eaten

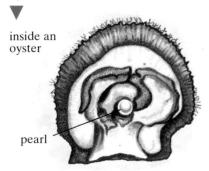

inside an
oyster

pearl

Pp

pace 1. one step in walking
2. speed (He walked at a brisk
pace.)

pacifist someone who does not believe
in war

pack 1. a group of things (a pack of
cards)
2. to put things into a container
(You pack a case.)
package, packet, packing

paddle 1. a short oar for a canoe
2. to walk in shallow water
paddling, paddler

paddock a field

page 1. one side of a sheet of paper in a
book
2. a boy messenger in a hotel

pageant an entertainment based on
historical events

pagoda a sacred tower in the Far East

pail a bucket

pain the unpleasant feeling when your
body hurts
painful, painfully, painless

paint a liquid used for colouring things

painter, paint-box, paint-brush
pair a set of two (a pair of gloves)
palace a large house for a ruler or
   bishop
pale having little colour (pale blue)
palm 1. the flat front of your hand
   2. a tree (See page 145)
pancake a thin flat cake fried in a pan
panda a black and white bear-like
   animal
   panda-car, panda-crossing

▼

pane a piece of glass in a window
panic sudden fear that makes you
   behave stupidly
   panicked, panicking, panicky
pansy a small flower
   pansies
pant to take quick short breaths
panther a kind of leopard
pantomime a play about a fairy-story
   at Christmas time
pants 1. underclothing
   2. trousers in US English
paper material used for writing on and
   wrapping up things
   paperback
parable a story that teaches a lesson

parachute a cloth device to break
   someone's fall when they jump
   from an aircraft
   parachuting, parachutist
parade a public march
paraffin an oil used as fuel
paragraph a section of writing dealing
   with one topic only
parakeet a kind of small parrot (See
   below)
parallel (Parallel lines are always the
   same distance apart, like railway
   lines.)
parasite a plant or animal that lives on
   another
paratroops troops trained to drop
   from aircraft by parachute
parcel something wrapped in paper
   and fastened
   parcel post, parcelled
pardon to forgive
   pardonable, pardonably, pardoned
parent a mother or father
   parental, parenthood
park 1. an open space set aside for
   people to enjoy themselves
   2. to leave your car
   car park, parking-meter
parliament the meeting place for the
   people chosen to make the laws of
   the country
parrot a bird

▼

parakeet

parrot

parsley a green herb
parsnip a root vegetable
part 1. a piece; a share
 2. to separate
particular special; this one and not the
 others
partner one of two people who do
 things together
 partnership
party a group of people having fun (a
 birthday party)
 parties
pass 1. to go by; to overtake
 2. to hand (Please pass the bread.)
 3. a gap between two mountains
 4. to get through an exam or test
 5. a permit that lets you pass
 through
 passable, passer-by, passport,
 pastime, password
passage 1. a narrow way through
 2. a piece of writing taken from a
 book
passenger a person taken by car, train,
 ship or aircraft
past 1. the time gone by
 2. after (It is past your bedtime.)
paste 1. a thick liquid for sticking
 things together
 2. any soft wet mixture
pastry a mixture of flour, water and fat
 for cooking
pasture grassland for feeding animals
pat to touch gently
 patted, patting
patch a piece of material put over a
 hole
 patches, patchy, patchwork

path a narrow track for walking along
patient 1. able to wait without
 complaining
 2. a person who is being treated by a
 doctor
 patience, patiently
patrol to go about to see that all is well
 patrolled, patrolling, patrol car
pattern 1. something to copy (a dress
 pattern)
 2. a design that is repeated (the
 pattern on wallpaper)
pause a short stop or wait
 pausing
pavement a path of flat stone at the
 side of the street
paw the foot of an animal with claws
pay to give money for something
 paid, payment
pea a vegetable that grows in a pod
 (See page 151)
peace 1. a time when there is no war
 2. a time that is calm and quiet
 peaceful, peacefully, peacefulness
peach a juicy fruit (See page 59)
peacock a large bird with beautiful
 feathers *peahen*

peahen

peacock

peak 1. the highest part of something (a mountain peak)
2. the hard front part of a cap

peanut a groundnut

pear a juicy fruit (See page 59)

pearl a precious stone found in an oyster (See page 95)

peasant a person who works on the land in a small way

peat a kind of earth found in a bog

pebble a rounded stone often found on beaches

peck to bite or pick up food with the beak

peculiar strange; odd
peculiarly, peculiarity

pedal the part of a machine worked by the foot (a bicycle pedal)
pedalled, pedalling, pedaller

pedestrian a person who is walking
pedestrian crossing

peel 1. the skin of fruit or vegetables
2. to take off the skin

peep to take a quick look

peer to look closely

peg a clip to hold things (a clothes peg)
pegged, pegging

pen 1. a tool for writing in ink
2. an enclosed space (a sheep pen)
pen-friend, penning, penned

penalty a punishment for breaking the rules
penalties, penalty goal, penalize

pencil a tool for writing or drawing
pencilled, pencilling, pencil sharpener

pendulum a weight on a rod that swings backwards and forwards

penguin a bird from the Antarctic that ▶ cannot fly

penknife a small knife with blades that fold into the handle

penny a coin; 1-100th pound
pennies, pence, penniless, penny-farthing

pentagon a shape with five equal sides

people men, women and children

pepper 1. a hot powder for flavouring
2. a red or green vegetable

perch 1. a bird's resting place
2. to sit on something like a bird
3. a fresh-water fish

perfect having nothing wrong
perfectly, perfection

perform to do something; to act in a play
performer, performance

perfume scent; any sweet smell

perhaps maybe; possibly

peril great danger
perilous, perilously

period a length of time
periodical, periodically

emperor penguins

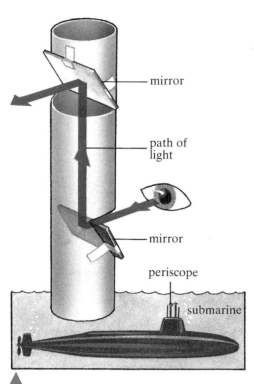

mirror

path of light

mirror

periscope

submarine

periscope an instrument for seeing around corners

perish to die or rot
perishable

permit to allow; a ticket allowing you to do something
permitted, permitting, permission

persist to go on doing something
persistent, persistence

person a man, woman or child
personally

perspire to sweat
perspiring, perspiration

persuade to make someone do something or believe something by talking
persuading, persuasion, persuasive

pessimist a person who expects the worst to happen
pessimism

pest any creature that causes trouble
pester

pet an animal you look after at home
petting, petted

petal one of the coloured parts of a flower

petrol the liquid used to drive cars

pheasant a game bird

pheasant

golden pheasant

phalanger a marsupial mammal

phone short for telephone
phoning

photograph a picture made by a camera
photographer, photography

phrase a group of words used together ('In the morning' and 'under the tree' are both phrases.)

piano a musical instrument with a keyboard
pianos, pianist

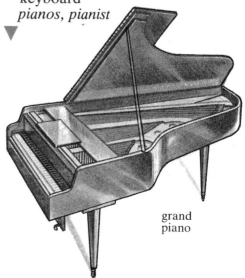

grand piano

pick 1. to choose
2. to take flowers from where they are growing
3. a tool for breaking up hard ground
pickaxe, pickpocket, pick-up

pickle food such as onions kept in vinegar

picnic a meal eaten out of doors
picnicked, picnicking, picnicker

picture a drawing, a painting or a photo

pie meat or fruit baked in pastry

piece a part of something

pier a long structure going out over the sea

pig an animal kept for its meat
piglet, pigsty, pigtail

saddleback

large white

landrace

pigeon a bird often found in towns

pigmy a very small person
pigmies

pike 1. a fresh-water fish with sharp teeth
2. a long spear

pile a heap of things

pilgrim a person who makes a journey to a holy place
pilgrimage

pill medicine made into a small flat round tablet

pillar a stone post for supporting a building
pillar-box

pillow a cushion for your head in bed

pilot a person who steers aircraft or guides boats into harbour

pimple a spot on your skin

pin a sharp metal fastener
pinned, pinning, safety-pin

pinafore a kind of apron
pinny

pincers a tool for gripping (See page 141)

pinch to squeeze with your fingers

pine 1. a family of evergreen trees with needle leaves (See page 146)
2. to long for something
pining

pineapple a large juicy fruit (See page 59)

pink a pale red colour

pint a measure of liquid; 0.57 litre
pioneer a person who is the first to do
something
pipe 1. a tube to carry gas or liquid
2. a tube with a bowl for smoking
3. a simple flute
pipeline, piper, piping
pirate a robber at sea
piracy, piratical
pistol a small gun held in the hand
pit a hole in the ground
pitch 1. an area marked out for a game
2. the highness or lowness of a note
3. tar used for road-making
4. to throw (He pitched the ball
short.)
5. to set up a tent
pitches, pitchfork
pity a feeling of sadness for someone
*pitied, pities, pitying, pitiful,
pitifully, pitiless, pitilessly*

place any area or position; a village,
town or district
placing
plague a serious infectious disease
plaice a flat sea fish (See page 55)
plain 1. easy to understand
2. without decoration
3. a large flat area of land
plait hair twisted into a rope
plan 1. something you have arranged
to do
2. a diagram of what something
looks like from above
planned, planning, planner
plane 1. a short way of saying
aeroplane
2. a tool for smoothing wood (See
page 141)
3. a tree with flaking bark
planet a heavenly body that goes
round the sun

Mercury
Venus
Earth
Mars
Jupiter
Saturn
Uranus
Neptune
Pluto

plank a long flat piece of wood

plant 1. anything that grows in the ground
2. to put something in the ground to grow

plaster 1. a mixture to cover walls
2. a piece of material to cover a wound

plastic a man-made material

plasticine a soft material for making models

plate a flat dish for putting food on

platform 1. a raised floor; a stage
2. the raised part of a railway station from which people get on and off the train

play 1. to have fun; not to work
2. a story acted on a stage
3. to take part in a game
4. to use a musical instrument
player, playful, playground,
playing-field, playtime, play-back

pleasant enjoyable; nice

please 1. to make someone happy
2. the polite word used when asking for something
pleasing

pleasure happiness; fun

pleat a fold made in material

plenty more than enough
plentiful, plentifully

pliers a tool for gripping things (See page 141)

plot 1. a secret plan
2. what happens in a story
3. a piece of ground for building on
plotted, plotting, plotter

plough a tool for turning over soil

plug a stopper for a hole

plum a kind of fruit with a stone

plumber someone who fits and repairs water pipes

plump rather fat

plunge to jump or put into a liquid
plunging, plunged, plunger

plural more than one

plus added to; the sign + (4+3=7)

poach 1. to cook gently in water
2. to catch animals on someone's land without permission
poaches, poacher

pocket a place in your clothes to carry things
pocket-knife, pocket-money

pod a seed case for peas, beans, etc.

poem a set of written lines with rhythm and often with rhymes
poet, poetry, poetic

point 1. the sharp end of something
2. to show something with your finger
3. a single in a score

4. a dot
pointer, pointless, point-blank

poison something that causes harm or death when swallowed
poisonous, poisonously, poisoner

polar to do with the North or South Poles
polar bear

pole a long round piece of wood or metal

police the people who make sure the laws of the country are kept
policeman, policemen, policewoman, policewomen, police station

polish to make smooth and shining

polite having good manners; well-behaved
politely, politeness

pollen the yellow powder found in flowers

polythene a plastic material, often colourless

pond a small lake

pony a small kind of horse
ponies

pool a pond; a puddle

poor 1. having little money
2. not very good; badly done

pop 1. a sudden sharp sound
2. popular music
popped, popping

poppy a flower

popular liked by many people
popularity

population the number of people living in a place

porch a roofed place outside the entrance

New Forest pony

Connemara pony

Exmoor pony

Shetland pony

103

porcupine a prickly wild animal

pore a tiny hole in the skin through which sweat passes

pork the meat from pigs

porpoise a sea mammal like a small whale

porridge a breakfast food made from oats

port 1. a place where ships unload
2. a kind of red wine
3. the left-hand side of a ship

porter a person who carries luggage

portion a part or share

portrait a picture of a person

position the place where something is

positive certain; sure

possess to have something; to own it
possesses, possession, possessor

possible able to be done or happen
possibly, possibility, possibilities

post 1. a piece of wood or metal fixed in the ground
2. letters and parcels; mail
post office, postage, postal, postcard, postman, postmark

poster a large sheet of paper with writing and pictures to inform people

potato a root vegetable (See page 151)
potatoes

pottery things made from clay

poultry farm birds such as hens and ducks

pound 1. a measure of weight; 0.45 kilograms
2. a unit of money
3. to hit again and again

pour to make liquid run out steadily

powder anything crushed into dust

power strength
powerful, powerfully

practice 1. the doing of something
2. all of a doctor's patients

practise to do something again and again (You should practise the piano everyday.)
practising

prairie a huge area of grassland, particularly in the USA

praise to speak well of something
praising, praiseworthy

pram a carriage for a baby

prawn a shellfish like a big shrimp (See page 119)

pray 1. to talk to God
2. to ask earnestly
prayer, prayer-book

preach to talk about right and wrong

precious worth a lot

precipice a very steep and high cliff

prefer to like one better than the other
preferable, preferably, preference, preferred, preferring

prehistoric before history was written down

prepare to get ready
preparing, preparation

present 1. a gift
2. now (the present time)
3. here; not absent

presently soon; in a moment

preserve to keep in good condition

president the chief person of a country, a club, a business

press 1. to push steadily
2. to smooth (You press clothes.)
3. a printing machine
presses, pressure, press gang

pretend to make believe
  pretence
pretty pleasant to look at
  prettier, prettiest, prettiness, prettily
prevent to stop something from
  happening
  prevention
previous earlier in time
prey an animal hunted by another
price what you have to pay for
  something
  priceless, pricing
prick to make a hole with something
  pointed
prickle a thorn
  prickly
pride the feeling of having done
  something well
  proud
priest a religious leader
primary first; most important
  primarily
primrose a wild flower

prince the son of a king or queen
princess the daughter of a king or
  queen
print to put words on paper with a
  machine
  printer, printing press
prison a place where criminals are kept
  prisoner
private 1. not public; for your own use
  only
  2. the lowest rank of soldier
prize something given to the winner

probable likely to be or to happen
  probably, probability
problem something difficult to do
produce to bring into being or into
  view
  producer, producing, production
profit the money you make in selling
  something for more than you paid
  for it
  profitable, profitably
programme 1. a list of things to be seen
  or heard at a concert or play
  2. any show or item on the radio or
  television
progress to go forward; to make
  headway
  progressive, progression, progresses
promenade a place for walking, often
  by the sea
promise to say you will do something
  promising
prompt at the right time
  promptly, promptness
prong one of the pointed pieces at the
  end of a fork
pronoun a word used instead of a noun
  (He, she, it, them are all pronouns.)
pronounce to say words aloud
  pronouncing, pronunciation
proof something that shows what the
  truth is
prop to stop something from falling
  propped, propping
propeller blades that turn to drive an
  aircraft or ship

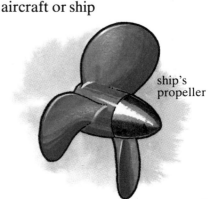

ship's
propeller

105

proper right; suitable
properly
property land and buildings that you own
prophet a person who says what will happen in the future
prophecy, prophesies, prophesied, prophetic
prosecute to take someone to court
protect to look after or guard
protection, protective, protector
proud pleased about something you have done well
proudly
prove to show that something is true
proverb an old wise saying
proverbial
provide to supply
prune a dried plum
psalm a song from the Bible
public for the use of people in general
pudding the sweet course of a meal
puddle a small pool of water
puffin a sea bird

pull to try to move something towards you
pullet a young hen
pullover a knitted garment; a jersey
pulp a soft wet mass

pulpit a platform to preach from
pulse the beat as blood is pumped through your veins
pump a machine for forcing air or water along a pipe
pumpkin a large fruit growing on a vine and used to make jack-o'lanterns at Halloween

jack-o'lantern

punch 1. to hit with your fist
2. to make holes with a machine
punctual at the right time; not late
punctuality, punctually
punctuate to put full stops, commas and other marks into your writing
punctuating, punctuation
puncture to make a small hole in something
punish to make someone suffer for

what he has done wrong
punishes, punishment
pupil 1. anyone who learns from a
teacher
2. the dark centre part of the eye
puppet a doll made to move either by
pulling strings or by moving the
fingers
puppy a young dog
purchase to buy
purchasing, purchases
pure not mixed with anything else
purely, purified, purifying, purity
purple a dark colour made by mixing
red and blue
purpose the aim; what you intend to
do
purposely, purposeful
purr to make a sound like a happy cat
purse a small bag to keep money in
pursue to chase after
pursuer, pursuing, pursuit
push to try to move something away
from you
pushchair, pushover
pussy a cat or a kitten
pussies
puzzle something to solve; a tricky
problem
puzzling
pyjamas a coat and trousers for
sleeping in
pylon a steel tower to carry cables
pyramid a shape with four sides and a
pointed top
python a large snake

Qq

quack to make a noise like a duck
quaint unusual in an attractive way
qualify to have the right training,
age, certificates for the job,
competition, etc.
qualified, qualifies, qualification
quality the goodness or condition of a
thing
quantity the amount of something
quantities
quarrel to disagree and argue angrily
quarrelled, quarrelling, quarrelsome
quarry a place where building stone is
dug
quart a measure of liquid; two pints
(1.14 litres)
quarter one of four equal parts of a
whole; the sign ¼
quay a landing place for boats
queen the female ruler of a country or
the wife of a king
queer odd; unusual
question something asked and needing
an answer
question mark, questionable
questionnaire a list of questions to be
answered
queue a line of waiting people or cars
queuing
quick fast; with speed
quiet with little noise; still
quit to give up; to leave
quitted, quitting
quite 1. completely
2. rather
quiver 1. to tremble; to shake
2. a case for holding arrows
quiz a competition in which questions
have to be answered
quizzed, quizzing
quoits a game played with rings

Rr

rabbit a furry wild animal

race 1. a competition in which the fastest wins
2. a large group of people of the same kind and colour
race-course, race-horse, racing, racial

rack a frame for holding things

racket 1. a bat (a tennis racket)
2. a great noise (What a racket!)

radar a way of finding out where ships, aircraft, etc. are by using radio

radiator 1. something that gives out heat
2. the part of a car that keeps the engine cool

radio 1. sound sent through the air on electrical waves
2. an instrument for receiving these waves

radish a small red vegetable used in salads
radishes

radius a straight line from the centre of a circle to the circumference

raffia straw from palm leaves

raft a floating platform

rag a torn or old piece of cloth
ragged

rage great anger
raging, enraged

raid a surprise attack
raider

rail a long bar (the rails of a railway)

railing a fence made with rails

rain drops of water falling from clouds
rain-drop, raincoat, rainfall, rainy

rainbow the arch of seven colours seen when the sun shines through rain

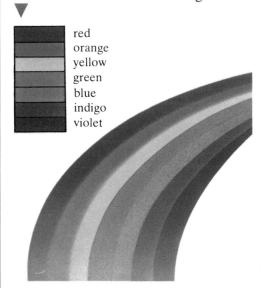

red
orange
yellow
green
blue
indigo
violet

raise to lift up; to bring up

raisin a large dried grape

rake a garden tool with teeth (See page 141)

ram 1. a male sheep
2. to push hard into something
rammer, ramming, rammed

ranch a large cattle farm

range 1. to vary between two limits (Prices ranged from £3 to £5.)
2. the distance a gun can shoot
3. a row of things (a mountain range)

rank a person's position in scale of importance

ransom the money demanded to set a prisoner free

rapid quick; swift
rapids, rapidly, rapidity
rare not often seen; not common
rarely, rareness, rarity
rascal a dishonest or naughty person
rash 1. acting without thinking
2. an outbreak of red spots on the skin
rashes, rashly, rashness
raspberry a soft red fruit (See page 59)
raspberries
rat a gnawing animal

brown rat

black rat

rather 1. fairly, somewhat (It is rather hot today.)
2. more truly (I would rather have a swim than a walk.)
ration the amount allowed
rattle to make short sharp shaking sounds
rattling, rattle-snake
rave 1. to shout wildly (raving mad)
2. to show a strong liking (He raved about the holiday he had.)
ravenous very hungry
ravine a deep narrow valley
raw 1. not cooked
2. sore and red
ray a narrow line of light
razor a sharp instrument used for shaving

reach 1. to get to; to arrive
2. to stretch out your hand to touch
reaches, reachable
read to understand written language
ready prepared
readily, readiness
real true, not imaginary
really, reality
realize to come to understand something
realise, realization, realizing, realism
reap to cut and gather crops
rear 1. the back (a rear seat)
2. to rise up on the back legs
reason why something is done
reasonable, reasonably
rebel to say you will not obey the leader
rebellious, rebellion
receipt a piece of paper saying something, such as money, has been received
receive to take what has been given
receiving, receiver
recent having happened a short time ago
recipe instructions for cooking food
recite to say aloud something learnt by heart
reciting, recitation
reckon 1. to count up
2. to consider
recognize to know something when you see it
recognizing, recognizable, recognise, recognition
recommend to speak well of something
recommendation
record 1. a disc played on a record-player
2. the best performance
3. an account of what has happened
recorder a musical instrument (See page 90)

recover 1. to get something back
2. to get better after an illness
recovered, recovery

recreation games and other things you do in your spare time

rectangle a four-sided shape with square corners
rectangular

red a colour; the colour of blood

reduce to make smaller
reducing, reduction

reed a tall grass growing near water

reef a line of rock or coral just below or just above the sea

reel 1. something to wind cotton or film on to
2. a Scottish dance
3. to walk unsteadily

refer 1. to mention (He didn't refer to what happened.)
2. to turn to something for information (He referred to his Atlas to find Tibet.)
referred, referring, reference

referee someone who sees the rules are obeyed, usually in a game

reflect 1. to shine back as from a mirror
2. to think hard
reflector, reflection

refreshment something to eat or drink

refrigerator a cupboard for keeping food cold
refrigerate, refrigeration

refuse to say 'no' to something
refusing, refusal

regiment a large unit in the army, commanded by a colonel
regimental

region an area of a country or the world

register 1. a list of names
2. to record information officially (You can register a letter at the Post Office.)

regret to be sorry

regretful, regrettable, regretted, regretting

regular happening steadily or at equal spaces of time
regularly, regularity

reign the time that a king or queen rules

reindeer a large deer with antlers

reins straps used to guide a horse

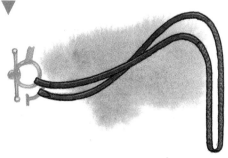

rejoice to show you are happy about something
rejoicing

relation or **relative** someone in the same family, such as an aunt, a cousin
related, relationship

relay race a race in which teams compete

reliable able to be trusted

relief something which brings the end of trouble
relieve, relieving

religion the belief in God
religious, religiously

rely to trust in; to depend on
relies, relied, reliable

remain 1. to stay behind
2. to be left over
remainder

remark to observe; to speak about
remarkable, remarkably

remedy a cure
remedies

remember to keep in your mind so as not to forget

remind to make someone remember
remove to take away
removing, remover, removal, removable
rent the money paid for the use of a house
repair to mend; to put right
repeat to say or do something again
repeatable, repetition
repent to be sorry for what you have done
repentance, repentant
replace 1. to put back in its place
2. to put in the place of something else
replacing, replacement
reply to answer
replies, replied
report 1. to tell about something that has happened
2. the noise of gunfire; a bang
reptile an animal with cold blood and short legs or none
republic a country that is governed by a president rather than a monarch
request to ask for politely
require to need
requiring, requirement
rescue to get someone out of danger
rescuing, rescuer
resemble to look like something else
resembling, resemblance
reserve to keep something till needed
reserving, reservation
reservoir a specially-made lake for storing water
respect to admire people because of what they do
respectful, respectfully, respectable
rest 1. to stop working
2. the others; what is left
restaurant a place where you can buy and eat meals
result 1. something that happens because of something else

2. the answer to a sum; the final score in a game
retire to give up working because of age
retiring, retirement
retreat to go back
return 1. to go back to a place
2. to give back (Please return it after use.)
reveal to show or make known
revelation
revenge to do someone harm because of what was done to you
revenging, revengeful
reverse 1. to go backwards
2. to turn something the other way
reversing, reversible, reversal
revise to go over something again, often to pass a test
revising, revision
revolt to turn against the leader
revolution a revolt that overturns the government
revolutionary
revolve to turn like a wheel
revolver a kind of pistol that has a revolving holder for several shots
reward a present for a good deed
rhinoceros a large wild animal

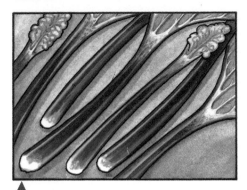

rhubarb a plant whose stalks can be eaten

rhyme to have the same end sounds (The word 'tall' rhymes with 'small'.)

rhythm the steady beat of poetry or music
rhythmic, rhythmical, rhythmically

rib one of the bones of your chest

ribbon a narrow band of material

rice a food grain grown in hot countries (See page 29)

rich having a lot of money

rid to make yourself free of something
ridded, ridding, riddance

riddle a word puzzle

ride to be on something (a horse, a car)
riding, rode, rider, ridden

ridiculous deserving to be laughed at

rifle a hand gun with a long barrel

right 1. the opposite of left
2. correct

rim the edge of wheels, cups, etc.

rind the hard outer skin (bacon rind)

ring 1. a circle
2. something the shape of a circle (a diamond ring)
3. to make a sound like a bell
ring-road, ringleader

rink a place made for skating

rinse to wash in clean water
rinsing

riot noisy violent behaviour by a crowd
rioter, riotous, riotously

rip to tear badly
ripped, ripping, ripper

ripe ready for eating
ripen, ripeness

ripple a very small wave
rippling

rise 1. to go up higher
2. to get up from bed
3. an increase in wages
rising, rose, risen

risk a chance, often dangerous

rival someone who tries to do better than you
rivalled, rivalling, rivalry

river a large stream of water flowing towards the sea

road a way made for traffic

roam to wander

roar to make a loud noise like a lion

roast to cook meat in an oven

rob to steal
robbed, robbing, robber, robbery

robe a long flowing garment

robin a garden bird with a red breast

rock 1. a large piece of stone
2. to move from side to side
3. a hard stick of sweet
4. a kind of music
rocking-chair, rocking-horse, rockery

rocket 1. a firework that shoots up into the air
2. a device for sending up spacecraft
rod a long thin bar
rodent an animal that gnaws
rodeo a riding show by cowboys
rogue a rascal; a cheat
roguery, roguish
roll 1. to turn over and over like a ball
2. a list of names (You call the roll.)
3. a small round piece of bread
4. something the shape of a tube (a roll of paper)
rolling-pin, roller-skates, rolling-stock
roof the covering of a house or vehicle
rook a large black bird (See page 21)
room 1. a division of a house
2. space to put things
root the underground part of a plant
root vegetables
rope a thick line made by twisting thinner ones together
rose a garden flower
rosy
rot to go bad
rotted, rotting, rotten, rottenness
rough 1. not smooth; uneven
2. not calm; stormy
round 1. the shape of a circle or ball
2. surrounding (There is a hedge round our garden.)
3. one stage in a competition
roundabout 1. a traffic island at the centre of a busy crossroads
2. something at a fair which goes round and round; a merry-go-round
rounders a game played with a bat and ball
row — rhyming with 'go' — 1. a line of things
2. to move a boat with oars
row — rhyming with 'now' — a great noise; a quarrel

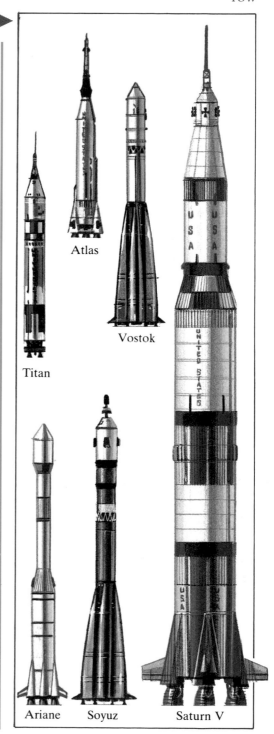

Atlas

Vostok

Titan

Ariane   Soyuz   Saturn V

113

royal to do with a king or queen
royally, royalty

rub to move one thing backwards and forwards against another
rubbed, rubbing, rubber

rubber 1. material made from the sap of the rubber tree
2. a piece of this to rub out pencil marks

rubbish 1. anything of no further use
2. nonsense (Don't talk rubbish!)

rudder the part used to steer a ship or plane

rude bad-mannered; not polite
rudely, rudeness

rug 1. a small carpet
2. a kind of blanket

rugby a kind of football played with an oval ball

ruin 1. what is left of an old building
2. to spoil something completely
ruinous, ruination

rule 1. to govern
2. a law
3. to draw a straight line with a ruler

ruler 1. a person who rules or governs
2. a stick for drawing lines

rumour something passed on as news, but which may not be true

run to move quickly
ran, runner, running, runny, runway

rung one of the bars of a ladder

rush to hurry; to move very quickly

rust a reddish-brown coating on iron left in the wet
rusty, rustiness

rustle to make a soft noise like wind in trees
rustling

rut a groove made by a wheel

ruthless cruel; without pity
ruthlessness

rye a cereal (See page 29)
ryebread

Ss

sack a large coarse cloth bag

sacred holy

sacrifice something you like and give up for a reason

sad unhappy
sadden, sadder, saddest

saddle a seat for a rider

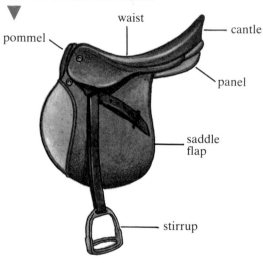

waist — cantle
pommel — panel
saddle flap
stirrup

safari a journey to see or hunt big game

safe 1. out of danger
2. a strong box for keeping valuables
safely, safety, safety-pin

sail 1. a sheet of cloth to catch the wind on a boat
2. to travel by boat; to steer a boat
sailor, sailing-ship

saint a holy person; someone who behaves very unselfishly
saintly, saintliness

salad a mixture of vegetables such as lettuce and cucumber eaten cold

salary a monthly wage

sale 1. the selling of anything for

money
2. the time when shops reduce prices
salesman, salesmen
salmon a large fish (See page 55)
salt a flavouring for food
salty, saltiness
salute to greet respectfully, like a
soldier
saluting
same alike; not different
sampan a Chinese flat-bottomed boat

satellite 1. a heavenly body that moves
round a planet
2. a man-made object that moves
round a planet
satisfy to make someone pleased
satisfied, satisfies, satisfactory
Saturday the seventh and last day of
the week
sauce a liquid used to flavour food
saucepan a metal cooking pot with lid
and handle
saucer a small dish to put a cup on
sausage a meat mixture usually put
into a skin
savage fierce; wild, angry
save 1. to keep for later use
2. to help someone in danger
saving, savings
saw a tool for cutting wood (See page
141)
sawdust, sawyer
saxophone a musical instrument

sample a small part to show what the
whole is like
sand powdered stone
sandy, sandiness, sand-storm
sandal an open shoe held on with
straps
sandwich two slices of bread with meat
or other food as a filling
sandwiches
sane having a normal mind; not mad
sanely, sanity
sap the juice in a living plant
sardine a small fish often tinned (See
page 55)
satchel a bag hung from the shoulder
for carrying school books

say to produce words with the voice
  said, saying
scab a dry crust formed on a wound
scaffolding platforms for builders to
  stand on when working high up
scale 1. a set of musical notes
  2. one of the hard flakes on the skin
  of a fish
  scaly
scales a machine for weighing
scamper to run quickly like a mouse
scar the mark left after a wound has
  healed
  scarred
scarce not plentiful; hard to find
scare to frighten
  scaring, scarecrow
scarf a long piece of cloth worn round
  the neck
  scarves
scarlet bright red
scatter to throw in different directions
scene 1. a place where something
  happens
  2. a view
  3. a division of a play
  scenery
scent 1. a sweet smell
  2. a liquid used to make people
  smell nice
scholar someone who is learning
school a place for teaching and
  learning
  schoolboy, schoolgirl,
  schoolteacher, schoolmaster,
  schoolmistress
schooner a large sailing-ship
science knowledge that comes from
  making experiments
  scientist, scientific
scissors an instrument with two blades
  for cutting
scone a small bun
scooter 1. a small motor cycle
  2. a two-wheeled toy

scorch to burn slightly
score 1. the number of points in a game
  2. to win a point in a game
  3. twenty
  score-board, scorer, scoring
scorn to treat as worthless; to despise
  scornful, scornfully
scorpion a small stinging animal like a
  spider

scoundrel a bad person; a rogue
scout 1. someone sent to find out
  about the enemy
  2. a member of the Boy Scouts
scramble 1. to move over rough
  ground on hands and feet
  2. to beat eggs and then cook them
  scrambling, scrambler, scrambled
scrap 1. a small piece of something
  2. rubbish
  3. a fight
  scrapped, scrapping, scrap-book
scrape to rub with a rough edge
  scraper, scraping
scratch 1. to mark with something
  sharp
  2. to rub yourself where it itches
  scratches, scratcher
scream to make a loud high cry
screen a frame covered with material
screw a kind of nail with a special
  groove that goes into wood by being
  turned
  screw-driver, cork-screw
scribble to write badly and hurriedly
  scribbling, scribbler

scrub to wash with a hard brush
scrubbed, scrubbing, scrubber
sculptor someone who carves things in stone or wood
sculpture
sea the salt water that covers most of the earth
seagull, seashell, seaside, seaweed

seagull

elephant seal

fur seal

seaweed

seashells

seal 1. to fasten something so that it cannot be opened without breaking the fastening
2. a large furry sea animal
seam 1. the line where two pieces of material are sewn together
2. a layer of coal underground
search to try to find by looking hard
season 1. a part of a year (Autumn is a season, and we speak of the football season.)
2. to add salt, pepper, etc., to food.
seasonal, seasoning
seat something to sit on
second 1. the one after the first
2. a sixtieth of a minute
secret something kept from everyone except a very few
secretly, secrecy, secretive

secretary an office worker in charge of correspondence
secretarial
section a part of something
secure 1. safe
2. fixed or firm
securely, securing, security
see what you do when you use the eyes
saw, seen
seed the part left by a flower that will grow into a new plant
seedling, seedy
seek to look for
seem to appear to be
see-saw a plank on which children can sit and go up and down
seize to take hold eagerly
seldom not often; hardly ever
select to choose

117

selfish thinking only about yourself
selfishly, selfishness
sell to give for money
semicolon a punctuation mark (;)
semi-final a match played to decide who shall play in the final
send to make something go somewhere
sent, send-off
senior older or more important
sense 1. (Sight, hearing, taste, smell and touch are our five senses.)
2. what makes you behave wisely
3. meaning (It doesn't make sense.)
sensible wise; not silly
sensibly
sentence a group of words making complete sense and ending with a full stop (.)
sentry a soldier on guard
sentries, sentry-box
separate not together; apart
separately, separation, separable
September the ninth month of the year
sergeant a rank of soldier or policeman
serial a story told in parts
serious important; not joking
seriously, seriousness
sermon a religious talk
serpent an old-fashioned word for a snake
servant someone who is paid to work for someone else, usually in the house
serve 1. to give people food at table
2. to attend to customers in a shop
3. to play the first stroke in tennis
serving, server
service helping other people
serviette a piece of material to keep your clothes clean while eating; a napkin
settee a long seat for more than one person
seven the number 7

seventh
seventeen the number 17
seventeenth
seventy the number 70
seventies, seventieth
several more than two but not many
severe 1. strict
2. serious (a severe cold)
severely, severity
sew to make stitches with needle and thread
sewing-machine, sewn
shabby nearly worn out
shabbier, shabbiest, shabbily, shabbiness
shade 1. an area hidden from the light
2. to keep the light away
3. a cover for a light
4. to make a drawing darker with your pencil
shadow the dark shape made by an object when it gets in the way of a bright light
shake to move something quickly up and down or from side to side
shaken, shaking, shook, shaky, shakily
shallow not deep
sham 1. to pretend
2. false or faked
shammed, shamming
shame the bad feeling you get when you have done something wrong
shameful, shamefully, shameless
shampoo a liquid soap for washing the hair
shamrock a plant like clover
shape the form of a thing, its appearance
shaping, shapeless, shapely
share 1. to divide something out among several people
2. to use something which other people also use
sharing

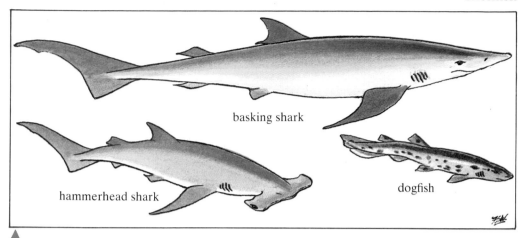

basking shark

hammerhead shark

dogfish

shark a large sea-fish
sharp 1. pointed; having a cutting edge
2. clever; bright
sharpen, sharpness
shave to cut off hair with a razor
shaving, shaver
shear to cut the wool off a sheep
shorn
shears large scissors for cutting
hedges, grass, wool etc.
shed a small building for storing things
sheep an animal kept for its wool and

meat
sheet 1. a large piece of material used
on a bed
2. any thin flat piece (a sheet of
paper)
shelf a board fixed to the wall for
holding things
shelves, shelving
shell 1. the hard outside covering of
eggs, nuts, shellfish etc.
2. a large bullet
shellfish any sea animal with a shell

Welsh
mountain
ram

blackface
ewe

southdown
ewe

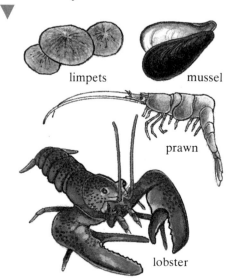

limpets

mussel

prawn

lobster

shelter a place where you are safe from the weather or danger

shepherd someone who looks after sheep

sheriff a person who sees that the laws are obeyed, especially in the USA

shield 1. a piece of armour carried to protect the body
2. to protect; to guard

Roman shield

halbadier

sports trophy

shift 1. to move
2. a group of people who work together at a particular time

shin the front of your leg below the knee

shine 1. to give out light
2. to make bright; to polish
shining, shiny, shone

shingle the small stones on a beach; pebbles

ship a large boat
shipper, shipping, shipwreck, shipyard

shirk to avoid work

shirt a garment with sleeves and a collar

shiver to shake with cold or fear

shoal a crowd of fish of the same sort

shock an unpleasant surprise

shoe a covering for the foot
shoelace, shoemaker

shoot 1. to fire a gun
2. to kick a ball at the goal
3. a new growth on a plant
shot, shooting star

shop a place where you buy things
shopkeeper, shopped, shopper, shopping

shore the land at the edge of the sea or a lake

short 1. not long in distance or time
2. not having enough; lacking (We are short of flour and must buy some more.)
shortage, shorten, short-sighted, shorthand

shorts knee-length trousers

shotgun a gun that fires many small lead balls or pellets

should ought to
shouldn't

shoulder the place where your arm joins your body
shoulder-blade, shoulder strap

shout to speak very loudly

shove to push
shoving

shovel a wide spade
shovelling

show 1. to let something be seen
2. to point out; to explain (I will show you what it means.)
3. an entertainment such as a play or exhibition

shower 1. rain falling for a short time
2. a device for spraying water on to the body

shriek to scream

shrimp a small shellfish

shrink to get smaller
shrank, shrinkage, shrinkable, shrunk

shrub a bush
shrubbery

shudder to shake from fear or horror

shunt to move railway trucks from one

track to another

shut 1. to close
2. not open
shutting, shutters

shy afraid to meet other people
shyly, shyness

sick 1. unwell
2. (To be sick also means to throw up your food.)
sickness, sickly, sickliness, sicken

side 1. one of the surfaces of a box, hill, piece of cloth, etc.
2. an edge (the side of the road)
3. one of two competing teams
sideboard, sidelights, side-show, sideways

sigh to breathe out heavily when sad, bored or tired

sight 1. a view; something seen
2. the power to see (poor sight)
sightseer, sightseeing, sightless

sign 1. to write your name
2. a notice that indicates something (a traffic sign)
3. something that has meaning (Black clouds are a sign of rain.)
signpost

signal to give a message by signs

signature your name written by yourself

silence the absence of all noise
silent, silently, silencer

silk a soft thread spun by silkworms

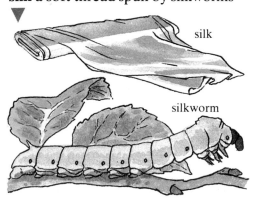

silk

silkworm

silly foolish; not sensible
sillier, silliest, silliness

silver a precious metal

similar almost the same; alike
similarity, similarly

simmer to boil, but only just

simple easy to do; plain
simplicity, simplify, simply

sin wickedness
sinned, sinner, sinning, sinful

since 1. after the time when (I have not seen him since we went swimming.)
2. because (We did not swim together since he did not come.)

sincere meaning what you say; genuine
sincerely, sincerity

sing to use your voice to make music
singer, sang, sung

single 1. only one
2. not married
singly, single-handed

sink 1. to go down, especially in water
2. a large bowl with taps and a drain
sank, sunk, sunken

sip to drink a tiny amount
sipped, sipping

siren a hooter used as a warning

sister a girl with the same parents as another child

sit to rest on your bottom
sat, sitting, sitter, sitting-room

six the number 6
sixth

sixteen the number 16
sixteenth

sixty the number 60
sixties, sixtieth

size how big something is
sizeable

skate 1. to move over ice wearing boots fixed with metal blades; to move over hard ground wearing roller skates
2. a fish
skating, skater

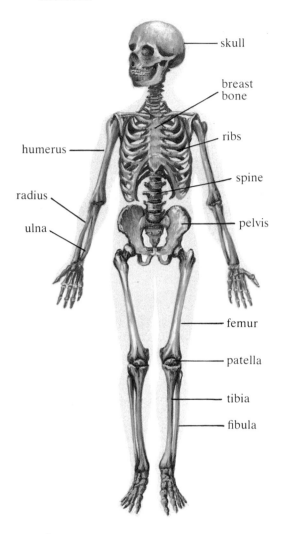

- skull
- breast bone
- ribs
- humerus
- spine
- radius
- ulna
- pelvis
- femur
- patella
- tibia
- fibula

▲

skeleton the bones of a body without the flesh

sketch a quick drawing
sketches, sketch-book

ski to move over snow on skis
skied, skier, ski-ing

skid to slide by accident on something slippery
skidded, skidder, skidding

skill the ability to do something well
skilful, skilfully

skin diver

▲

skin the outer covering of animals or fruit
skinny, skin-diving

skip 1. to jump over a rope that is being turned
2. to leave something out
skipped, skipping-rope

skipper the captain

skirt a garment for women and girls that hangs from the waist

skittles pieces of wood that can be knocked down with a ball

skull the bony part of your head

sky the open air high above you
skies, sky-diving, skylight, skyline

skylark a song-bird

▼

skyscraper a very tall building
slack 1. loose; not tight
2. not busy
3. careless, lazy
slacken, slackly, slackness
slacks trousers
slam to shut or hit with a great noise
slammed, slamming
slang language used among friends but
not on more formal occasions
slap to hit with the palm of your hand
slapped, slapping, slapper
slate a flat grey stone used on roofs
slaughter 1. to kill for food
2. to kill many at the same time
slave someone forced to work for a
master without pay
slaving, slavery
slay to kill
slain, slew
sledge a vehicle on runners to slide
over snow; a sled
sledge-hammer a very heavy hammer
sleep to rest with eyes closed
*sleeping-bag, sleepless, sleepy,
sleepiness, slept*
sleet falling snow that has almost
melted into rain
sleeve the part of a garment that covers
the arm
sleeveless
sleigh a sledge pulled by animals

slender not fat; slim; narrow
slice a flat piece cut off
slide 1. to move smoothly over a
slippery surface
2. a hair clip
slid, sliding
slight small; not important
slim not fat; thin
slimmer, slimmest, slimming
slime a slippery substance
slimy
sling 1. to throw
2. a device for throwing stones
3. material tied round the neck to
support an injured arm
slung
slip 1. to lose your balance and fall
2. a small mistake
slipped, slipping, slippery
slippers soft shoes worn indoors
slit a narrow opening
slog 1. to hit hard and wildly
2. to work very hard
slogged, slogging
slope ground that goes up or down
sloping

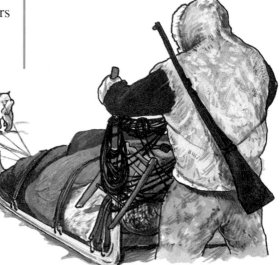

huskies

An arctic explorer
with a sleigh

123

sloppy

sloppy 1. wet; runny
  2. weak; careless; silly
  sloppily, sloppiness
slot a narrow opening to put
  something in
  slotted, slotting, slot-machine
sloth 1. laziness
  2. a South American animal
slouch to sit or move lazily
slow 1. not quick; taking a long time
  2. behind the right time
slug a small slimy garden creature

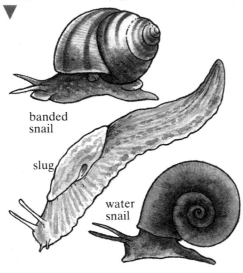

banded
snail

slug

water
snail

sly not to be trusted; crafty
  slyly, slyness
smack to hit with the open hand
small not big; little
smart 1. neat; well-dressed
  2. clever
  3. to sting
smash to break something into pieces
smell 1. to find out by using your nose
  2. to give off a smell
  smelly, smelt
smile to have a happy look on your
  face
  smiling, smiled, smiler
smoke the dark cloud that rises from
  something burning

*smoked, smoking, smoky,
  smokiness, smokeless*
smooth flat and even; without lumps
  smoothly, smoothness
smudge a dirty mark
smuggle to bring things into the
  country without paying tax
  smuggler, smuggling
snack a small quick meal
  snack-bar
snail a small creature with a shell on its
  back

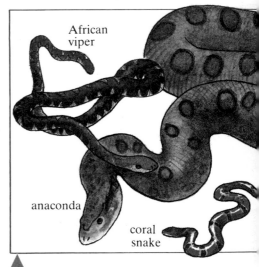

African
viper

anaconda

coral
snake

snake a long reptile without legs
snap 1. to break suddenly with a sharp
  sound
  2. to bite at angrily
  3. a snapshot; a photograph
  4. a card game
  *snapped, snapping, snapper,
  snappy, snappily*
snare a trap
snatch to grab; to try to get quickly and
  unexpectedly
sneak 1. to move quietly and secretly
  2. to tell tales
  sneaky, sneakily
sneer to talk as if you thought the
  person useless

124

sneeze to have a sudden noisy rush of air through your nose and mouth
sneezed, sneezing, sneezer

sniff to take a short breath through the nose as if smelling

snob a person who looks down on people without wealth or rank
snobbery, snobbish, snobbishly

snore to breath noisily when asleep

snorkel a tube enabling swimmers to breathe under the water
snorkelled, snorkelling

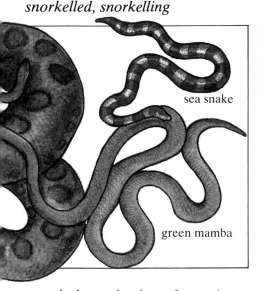

sea snake

green mamba

snow raindrops that have frozen into white flakes
snowball, snowdrop, snowflake, snowman, snowstorm

snug warm and comfortable

soak to make very wet

soap something used with water to wash
soapy, soapiness, soap-suds

sob to weep noisily
sobbed, sobbing

soccer Association Football

society 1. people living as one group or nation
2. a club
social, sociable, societies

sock a short covering for the foot

sofa a long seat like a settee

soft 1. not hard
2. quiet (soft music)
softly, softness, soften, softener

soil 1. the earth in which plants grow
2. to make dirty (Babies quickly soil their clothes.)

soldier someone paid to fight in an army

sole 1. the bottom part of your foot
2. a flat fish

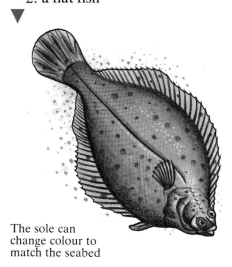

The sole can change colour to match the seabed

3. only (the sole person on the beach)

solemn very serious or thoughtful
solemnly, solemnity

solid with no space inside
solidly, solidity

solo 1. on your own (a solo flight)
2. a piece of music for one person only

solution 1. the answer to a problem
2. something dissolved in a liquid

solve to find the answer to a problem
solving, solvable

some a few; little; not all
somebody, somehow, someone, something, sometimes, somewhere

somersault to turn head over heels in the air

son someone's boy child
son-in-law, sons-in-law

song music for singing
songbird

soon in the near future

soot the black powder left by smoke

sore 1. painful
2. a painful place on your body

sorrow sadness; unhappiness
sorrowful

sorry 1. a polite word for apologising
2. feeling unhappy because you have done wrong
sorrier, sorriest

sort 1. to arrange into groups
2. a kind (What sort of animal is it?)

soul the part of a person that some believe to be immortal

sound 1. something that can be heard
2. in a good state
sound-barrier, sound-effects, soundless, sound-proof, sound-track

soup a liquid food

sour having a sharp taste; not sweet

source the place where something starts

south one of the points of the compass; opposite north
southerly, southern, southward, south-east, south-west

sow − rhyming with 'go' − to plant seeds

sow − rhyming with 'now' − a female pig

space 1. the distance between things; a gap
2. the place beyond the earth where there is no air
spacing, spacious, spacemen, spaceship, spacesuit

spade a tool for digging (See page 141)

spare 1. not being used

2. to be able to give (Can you spare me a sandwich?)

spark a tiny piece of light or flame
sparking-plug

sparkle to give off sparks of light
sparkler, sparkling

sparrow a small bird (See page 20)

speak to say something
speaker, spoke, spoken

spear a pointed weapon on a pole

special not ordinary; made for a particular use
specially, speciality

speck a tiny spot of dirt

spectacles glasses for seeing better

spectator someone who watches others doing something

speech 1. the sounds made when talking
2. a talk given on a special occasion
speeches, speechless

speed the rate at which something moves
speedy, speedily, sped, speedway, speed-boat, speedometer

spell 1. to give the letters that make up a word
2. words supposed to have magic power
spelling, spelt, spellbound

spend 1. to pay out money
2. to use up time (Tom spent a week in bed when he was ill.)

sphere a ball shape; a globe
spherical

spice strong-tasting food for flavouring

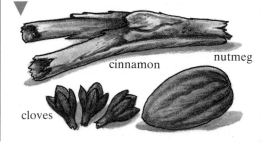

cinnamon

nutmeg

cloves

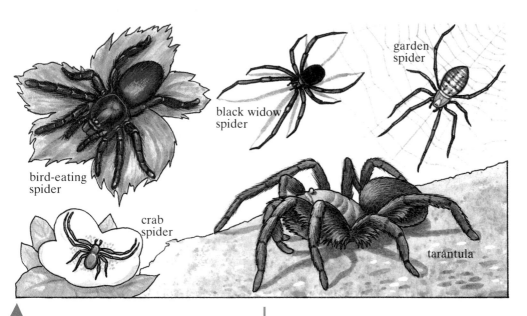

garden spider

black widow spider

bird-eating spider

crab spider

tarantula

spider a creature with eight legs that spins a web

spike a sharp point
spiky

spill to make something overflow

spin 1. to turn round and round
2. to make thread by twisting
spinner, spinning, spun, spin-drier

spine the backbone of an animal

spinster an unmarried woman

spire the pointed part of a church tower

spirit 1. the soul
2. a ghost
3. courage; liveliness
4. a strong drink

spit to force liquid out of your mouth
spat, spitting

spite ill-feeling; a desire to hurt
spiteful, spitefully, spitefulness

splash 1. to make water go over something
2. the noise made when something hits water
splashes, splash-down

splendid grand; excellent
splendidly, splendour

splinter a tiny sharp piece of something

split to cut or break from end to end
splitting

spoil to damage; to make useless
spoilt

spoke 1. a thin bar from the centre to the rim of a wheel
2. the past tense of 'to speak'

sponge 1. a sea animal
2. to cleanse or soak up water with a sponge
3. a soft kind of cake
spongy, sponging

spoon an instrument for eating or serving
spoonful

sport outdoor games or pastimes

spot 1. a small mark; a small amount; a pimple
2. to notice
spotted, spotting, spotty, spottiness

sprawl to sit or lie carelessly spread out

spray 1. to send out tiny drops of liquid
2. a bunch of flowers

spread 1. to stretch out (The bird spread its wings.)
2. to make something move out over a wide area (You spread a disease.)

spring 1. the season between winter and summer
2. a flow of water from the ground
3. to jump up suddenly
4. a coil of wire that springs
sprang, sprung, springy, spring-board, springtime

springbok a kind of South African antelope

sprint to run very quickly for a short distance

sprout to begin to grow and shoot out
brussels sprouts

spur a device fixed to the rider's heel to urge on a horse
spurred, spurring

spurt 1. a sudden rush of water
2. to speed up suddenly

spy someone who tries to find secret information
spies, spied, spy-catcher

squabble to have a noisy little quarrel
squabbling, squabbler

square a shape with four equal sides

squash 1. to squeeze
2. a fruit drink
3. a ball game

squat to sit on your heels
squatted, squatting, squatter

squeak a high sound like that of a mouse

squeal a long high cry of pain or joy

squeeze to press hard
squeezing, squeezer

squirrel a tree animal with a bushy tail

grey squirrel

red squirrel

squirt to send out a jet of water
stab to push something pointed into
   something
   stabbed, stabbing
stable a building where horses are kept
stack a large heap or pile
staff the people who work in a school,
   hospital, etc.
stag a male deer

ground
   2. to make a mark on something
   3. a small piece of paper to pay for
   postage
   stamp-album, stamp-collector
stand 1. to be upright on your feet
   2. rows of seats for spectators
standard of the normal quality
star 1. a large body in the sky seen as a

stage coach

stage 1. a platform for acting
   2. a section of a journey
   stage-coach
stagger 1. to sway as you walk
   2. to amaze
stain 1. a dirty mark
   2. to colour something such as wood
   stainless
stairs a number of steps leading from
   one floor to another
   staircase
stake a strong pointed post
stale old; not fresh
stalk 1. the stem of a flower or plant
   2. to follow an animal
stallion a male horse
stammer to hesitate and repeat sounds
   when talking
stamp 1. to bang the foot on the

point of light at night
   2. a famous actor or singer
starch 1. something found in food like
   bread and potatoes
   2.a powder made from this to stiffen
   clothes
   starchy, starchiness
stare to look continuously
   staring
starling a bird (See page 20)
start to begin
startle to surprise someone
   startling
starve to be ill because you have no
   food
   starving, starvation
state 1. the way something is; its
   condition
   2. a country or people under one

government
3. to say something clearly
stating, statement
station 1. a place where buses or trains stop
2. a place where people like policemen work
stationary not moving
stationery paper and writing materials
statue a figure usually carved from wood or stone
steady 1. firm; not shaking
2. regular; reliable
steadily, steadiness
steak a thick slice of meat or fish
steal to take what does not belong to you
steam the white cloud that appears when a liquid boils
steamy, steam-engine, steam-roller
steel a strong metal made from iron
steep going up or down sharply
steeply, steepness
steeple a tall pointed church tower
steer 1. to guide a vehicle
2. a young bull
steering-wheel
stem the part of a plant from which the leaves grow
step 1. a complete movement with one foot when you are walking
2. the place where you put your foot when walking from one level to another
stepped, step-ladder, stepping-stone
stern 1. strict; firm
2. the back end of a ship
stew meat cooked slowly with vegetables
stick 1. a long thin piece of wood
2. to join together with glue
sticky, stickiness
stiff 1. not easily bent (a stiff collar)
2. difficult (a stiff test)
stiffen, stiffly, stiffness

stile a step to help you over a fence
still 1. quiet; with no movement
2. up to this moment (He is still there.)
3. nevertheless
sting a small amount of poison pricked into the skin by a bee, nettle, etc.
stung
stingy mean; ungenerous
stingier, stingiest, stingily, stinginess
stir to move round and round with a spoon
stirred, stirring
stirrup a foot-rest for a horse-rider
stitch a small loop made when sewing
stitches
stock a supply ready to be drawn upon
stocking a long covering for the foot and leg
stoke to put fuel on a fire
stoker, stoking
stomach the part of your body where the food goes after eating
stone 1. a piece of rock
2. a jewel (precious stone)
3. the hard seed of fruit like plums
stony, stoniness, stonier, stone-deaf, stone-cold
stool a seat with no back
stoop to bend forwards and downwards
stop 1. to end what you are doing

2. to come to a halt
stopped, stopping, stoppage,
stopper
store 1. to put things away for later use
2. a large shop
storing, storage, store-room
storey all the rooms on one floor
stork large bird with long legs

storm rough wet weather
story words that tell about happenings
real or imaginary
stories, story-teller
stout 1. fat
2. thick and strong
stove 1. a cooker for food
2. a closed fire for heating
straight 1. with no bends; not crooked
2. with things in their right place
(Put the room straight, please.)
3. honest
straighten, straight-forward
strain 1. to stretch or pull hard
2. to injure by stretching
3. to separate the water from
anything cooked
strainer, strained muscle
strange unusual; not known
stranger, strangeness, strangely

strap a fastener made of leather with
a buckle
strapped, strapping
straw 1. the dried stems of corn
2. a tube for drinking through
strawberry a soft red fruit
strawberries

stray to wander away and get lost
stream a small river
street a road with houses
strength being strong; power
strengthen
stretch 1. to make longer by pulling
2. to reach out
stretches, stretchable
stretcher a covered frame for carrying
sick people
strict keen on good behaviour; stern
stride to walk with long steps
strike 1. to hit
2. to light (strike a match.)
3. to stop work because of a
complaint
striker, striking, struck
string thick thread for tying things
strip 1. a long narrow piece
2. to take off; to undress
stripped, stripping
stripe a long narrow mark
striped
stroke 1. to rub gently
2. a blow
stroking

131

stroll to walk along slowly

strong able to lift heavy things;
powerful

struggle to try hard to do something
difficult
struggling, struggler

study to learn
2. a room for quiet work
studied, studies, studious

stuff 1. a material
2. to fill with things

stumble to trip over and perhaps fall
stumbling, stumbler

stun 1. to knock unconscious
2. to amaze
stunning, stunned, stunner

stupid silly; foolish
stupidly, stupidity

stutter to hesitate and repeat sounds
while talking
stutterer

sty 1. a place where pigs are kept
2. a painful swelling on the eyelid
sties, styes

style the way of doing something
stylish

subject 1. a member of a particular
country (a British subject)
2. what is being talked or written
about (The main subject of the
book is ski-ing.)
3. a section of what is studied at
school (Maths is my favourite
subject.)

submarine a ship that can travel
underwater

substance anything that can be
touched; something used to make
things
substantial

subtract to take away
subtraction

succeed to do what you set out to do
success, successful, successfully

suck to draw something into the
mouth

sudden happening quickly and
unexpectedly
suddenly, suddenness

suffer to feel pain

sufficient enough

sugar a food added to make others
sweet
sugary, sugariness

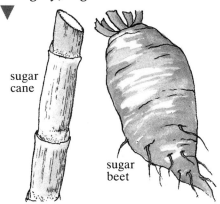

sugar cane

sugar beet

suggest to put forward an idea
suggestion, suggestive, suggestible

suit 1. a set of clothes
2. to be right for the person
suitable, suitably, suitcase

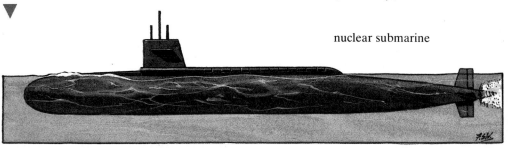

nuclear submarine

132

sulk to be silent and bad-tempered
sulky, sulkily, sulkiness
sultana a dried grape
sum 1. the total obtained when
numbers are added together
2. a problem in arithmetic
3. an amount of money
summer the season between spring
and autumn
summit the top of something
sun the body in the sky that gives the
earth light and heat
*sunbathe, sunbathing, sunbeam,
sunlight, sunflower, sunrise, sunset,
sunshine, sunny*
Sunday the first day of the week
superior better; higher in rank
superiority
supermarket a large shop where all
sorts of goods are on sale
supersonic faster than the speed of
sound
superstition belief in magic or chance;
belief in what does not stand up to
reason
superstitious
supper a light evening meal
supply to give what is wanted
supplies, supplied, supplier
support 1. to hold something up
2. to give help
suppose to guess; to imagine to be true
supposing, supposedly
sure knowing you are right
surely, sureness
surf white foaming waves breaking
surf-board

surface the outside or top of a thing
surgeon a doctor who operates on
people
surgical, surgery
surname your last or family name
surprise something that is not
expected
surprising, surprisingly
surrender to give up
surround to be all round something
swallow 1. to let food or drink go down
your throat
2. a small bird

swamp very wet soft ground
swan a large water-bird (See page 20)
swank to boast
swarm a very large number of insects
sway to move from side to side
swear 1. to make a solemn promise

surfer

surf-board

133

2. to curse; to use coarse language
swore, sworn, swear-word

sweat the wetness that comes from your body when you are too hot
sweaty, sweatiness

sweater a heavy knitted jersey

sweep 1. to clean with a brush or broom
2. a person who cleans chimneys

sweet 1. tasting like sugar; not sour
2. a small piece of something made mainly from sugar or chocolate
3. the pudding served at the end of a meal

swell to grow larger
swelling, swollen

swerve to move sideways suddenly
swerving

swift 1. fast
2. a small bird (See page 21)

swim to move through water using your arms and legs
swimmer, swimming, swam, swum, swim-suit

swing to move backwards and forwards without touching the ground

switch 1. a lever for turning electricity on or off
2. to change over

sword a weapon with a long sharp blade

syllable a word or part of a word containing only one vowel sound

sympathy the ability to understand and share people's feelings
sympathetic, sympathise

synagogue a building where Jews worship

syrup a thick sweet liquid

Tt

tabby a cat with striped fur

table a piece of furniture with legs and a flat top
table-cloth, tablespoon, table-tennis

tack 1. a small nail with a broad head
2. to sew quickly with long stitches
3. to sail a zig-zag course against the wind

tackle 1. to try to do something
2. things needed to do a job
tackling, tackler

tadpole a creature that grows into a frog, toad or newt

tag a label

tail the part at the end of something

tailor someone who makes clothes

take 1. to carry away; to remove
2. to get hold of (Take my hand.)
taken, taking, took

take-off the moment an aircraft leaves the ground

tale a story

talent any thing you are good at
talented

talk to speak
talkative

tall 1. high (a tall tree)
2. in height (He is six foot tall.)

talon the claw of a bird of prey

tame not wild or dangerous

tangerine a fruit like a small orange

tank 1. a large container for liquids
  2. an armoured car on tracks
tanker a ship or a truck carrying oil
tap 1. to hit gently
  2. a handle to turn on liquids, gas, etc.
  tapping, tapped
tape 1. a narrow strip of material
  2. to copy sound on a tape-recorder
  taping, tape-measure, tape-recorder
tar a sticky black substance for making roads
  tarry, tarred, tarring
target something at which you aim
tarmac the tarry surface of a road
tart 1. a piece of pastry filled with jam or fruit
  2. sour; sharp
  tartly, tartness, tartlet
tartan a material with a criss-cross pattern from Scotland
task a job; something to be achieved
tassel a hanging bunch of threads used as decoration
taste to recognize foods by using your tongue
  tasty, tastiness, tastier, tastiest, tasteless, tasteful

tax money paid to the government to pay for things used by everyone
  taxes
taxi a car you pay to ride in
tea 1. a drink made from the dried leaves of a bush
  2. an afternoon meal when tea is drunk
  tea-bag, teapot, tea-leaves, teaspoon, teatime, tea-tray

tea picker

tea plant

135

teach to give lessons; to show someone how to do something
taught, teacher, teachable

team a set of people who play or work together
team-work

tear — rhyming with 'bear' — to pull apart
tore, torn

tear — rhyming with 'fear' — a drop of water coming from your eye
tear-drop, tearful, tearfully

tease to make fun of someone
teaser, teasing

teddy-bear a toy bear

teenager a person aged from 13 − 19

telegram a short message sent by telegraph

telegraph a way of sending messages quickly by electricity

telephone an instrument enabling you to speak to people at a distance
telephoning, phone, phoning

telescope an instrument enabling you to see distant things more clearly

▼

television an instrument that brings pictures and sound through the air from great distances
telerecording, televise

tell to speak; to give news by speaking
tell-tale, told

temper the kind of mood you are in

temperature the measure of how hot or cold anything is

temple 1. the part between your forehead and ear
2. a building used for worship

tempt to try to persuade someone to do something he should not do
tempter, temptation

ten the number 10
tenth

tender 1. soft and easily hurt
2. loving (She looks after her baby with tender care.)

tennis a game played with rackets and a ball

optical telescope

radio telescope

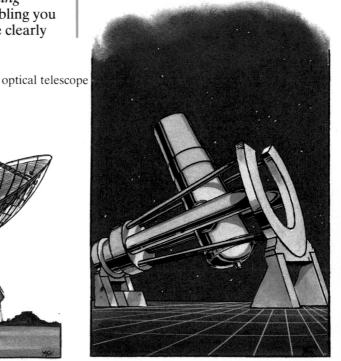

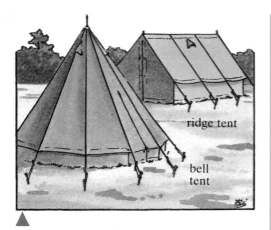

ridge tent

bell tent

tent a shelter made of canvas
term a period of time; part of a school year
termite a tropical insect like a large ant
terrace 1. a raised piece of ground
2. a row of houses joined together
terrible very bad; dreadful; frightening
terribly
terrier a kind of dog

Manchester terrier

fox terrier

Scottish terrier

Jack Russell

terrific 1. very great
2. excellent
terrifically
terrify to frighten very much
terrified, terrifies, terrifying
territory an area of land belonging to someone or to a country
territories
terror great fear
terrorist, terrorism, terrorize
test an examination; a try-out
test-match
text the words in a book
textbook
thank to say you are pleased and grateful
thankful, thankfully
thaw to become warmer weather so that the snow melts
theatre a building where plays are acted
theatrical

theft stealing
their belonging to them (their books)
theirs belonging to them (Those books are theirs.)
there in that place (Put them over there.)
therefore for that reason

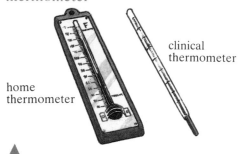

clinical
thermometer

home
thermometer

▲

thermometer an instrument to
measure temperature
thermos flask a container for keeping
drinks hot or cold
thick 1. wide; not thin
2. not flowing easily (a thick soup)
3. close together (a thick crowd)
thicken, thickness, thickly
thief someone who steals
thieves, theft
thigh the part of the leg above the knee
thimble a cover for the finger when
using a needle
thin narrow; not thick; not fat
thinner, thinnest, thinning, thinness
think to use your mind
thinker, thought
third the next after the second
thirsty wanting a drink
thirst, thirstily, thirstiness
thirteen the number 13
thirteenth
thirty the number 30
thirties, thirtieth
thistle a wild plant with prickly leaves

▼

thorn a sharp point on the stem of a
plant
thorough not leaving anything out
thoroughly, thoroughness
though even if (He is strong though
small.)
thought the act of thinking; an idea;
kindliness
*thoughtful, thoughtfully,
thoughtfulness, thoughtless,
thoughtlessly, thoughtlessness*
thousand the number 1,000
thousandth
thread 1. a long thin length of anything
2. to pass thread through the eye of
a needle
3. the raised line that goes round a
screw
threadbare
threat a warning of danger or trouble
threaten, threatening
three the number 3
third
thrill a feeling of excitement
thriller, thrilling
throat the inside front part of the neck
throb a steady beating sound or
movement
throbbed, throbbing
throne a special chair for a king or
queen
through from one end or side to the
other
throw to send something from the
hand into the air
threw, thrown
thrush a song-bird (See page 21)
thrushes
thumb the thick shortest finger
thunder the loud sound following
lightning
*thundery, thunderous,
thunder-storm, thunder-struck*
Thursday the fifth day of the week
tick 1. the sound made by a clock

2. the mark ✓ that shows something is right

ticket a small piece of paper to show you have paid to ride on a bus, see a show, etc.

tickle to touch someone's skin to make him laugh
tickling, ticklish

tide the rise and fall of the sea twice a day
tidal wave

tidy neat; carefully arranged
tidily, tidiness, tidier, tidiest, tidies

tie 1. to fasten with string
2. a strip of material worn round the neck
3. an equal score in a game
tying, tied

tiger a large fierce animal of the cat family
tigress

tight closely fitting; not loose
tighten, tight-fisted, tight-rope

tights a garment that covers the body from the waist down

tile a piece of baked clay for covering a roof or wall
tiling, tiler

till 1. to prepare soil for crops
2. up to; until (I waited till four o'clock for you)
3. money drawer in shop

timber wood used for building or furniture

time 1. the hour of the day shown on a clock
2. a period measured in minutes and hours
3. to measure how long it takes to do something
timing, timetable

timid easily frightened
timidly, timidity, timidness

tin 1. a silvery metal
2. a metal container; a can
tinned, tinny, tin-opener

tingle a prickly feeling on your skin
tingling

tinkle to make sounds like a small bell
tinkling

tinsel shiny strips of material used for decorating

tiny very small
tinier, tiniest, tininess

tip 1. the pointed end of something
2. to move on to one edge, to overturn
3. to give a small money present for a service
tipped, tipping, tiptoe

tired needing rest
tire, tiring, tiredness

title 1. the name of a book, poem, etc.
2. a word showing a person's rank or position (Dr, Sir, Lady, Lord are all titles.)

toad

common
toad

natterjack
toad

spadefoot
toad

giant
toad

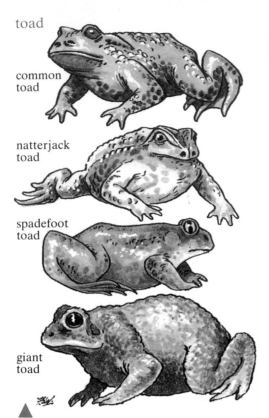

toad an animal like a large frog
toadstool kinds of fungus that are
   often poisonous

toast bread made crisp by heating
tobacco the dried leaves of a plant used
   for smoking
   tobacconist

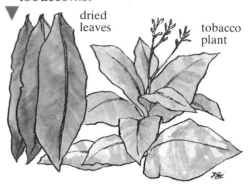

dried
leaves

tobacco
plant

toboggan a long narrow sledge
today this day
toddler a young child learning to walk
toe one of the five end parts of the foot
toffee a sticky sweet made from
   butter and sugar
together with someone or something
toilet a lavatory
tomahawk an axe used by American
   Indians

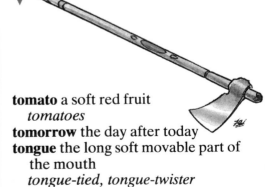

tomato a soft red fruit
   tomatoes
tomorrow the day after today
tongue the long soft movable part of
   the mouth
   tongue-tied, tongue-twister
tonight this night
tonne a measure of weight; 1,000
   kilograms
tonsils two small parts of the throat
   tonsilitis
tool something to help you do a certain ▶
   job

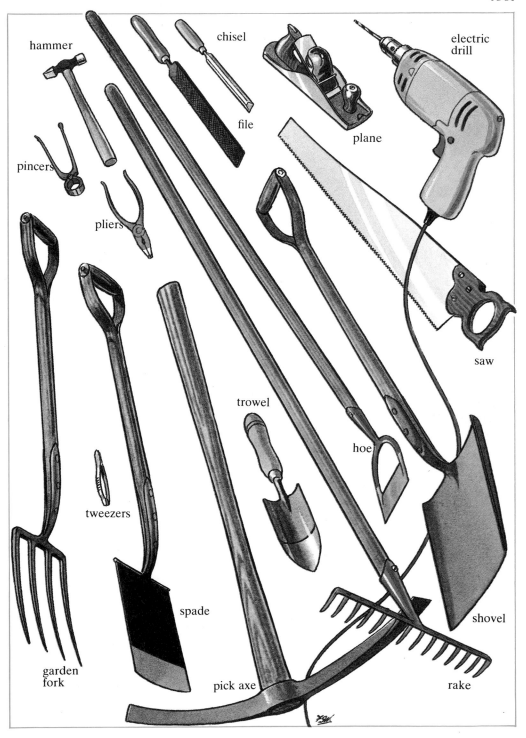

hammer

chisel

file

plane

electric drill

pincers

pliers

saw

trowel

hoe

tweezers

spade

shovel

garden fork

pick axe

rake

tooth one of the hard parts of the mouth used for biting
teeth, toothache, toothbrush, toothpaste

top 1. the highest part of something
2. a toy that spins
top-heavy, topless

torch an electric light you can carry
torches, torch-light

torpedo a large rocket-shaped bullet that travels through water
torpedoes

torrent a strong and fast flow of water
torrential

tortoise a slow-moving animal with a shell

torture to cause someone pain deliberately
torturer, torturing

toss to throw lightly into the air

total 1. everything added up
2. complete (a total collapse)
totalled, totalling, totally

touch 1. to feel something with the hand
2. to be so near that there is no space between
touches, touch-down, touch-line

tough strong; hard; difficult
toughness, toughen

tour a journey from place to place
tourist, tourism

tow to pull along a vehicle or boat
tow-bar, tow-rope, tow-path

towards in the direction of

towel a piece of cloth for drying
towelled, towelling, towel-horse

tower a tall building or part of one

town a place where a lot of people live close together

toy something to play with

trace 1. to copy something by drawing over it on thin paper
2. the mark left by something (The thief left no traces.)
tracing-paper, tracer

track 1. a rough path
2. marks left behind (the tracks of birds in the snow)
3. a road or path for racing
4. the metal band to drive tanks
5. to follow the tracks of someone
tracker, railway track

tractor a vehicle for pulling heavy loads

trade 1. the buying and selling of things
2. the kind of work people do (John's trade is plumbing.)
trader, tradesman, trading

traffic moving cars and other vehicles
traffic lights, traffic warden

trail 1. tracks; traces
2. to pull something along behind
trailer

train 1. carriages and engine on a railway
2. to learn a job; to practise

traitor someone who gives away secrets to the enemy

tram an electric bus running on lines
tramlines

tramp 1. a homeless person wandering from place to place begging
2. a long walk

trampoline canvas on a large frame used for gymnastics

transfer to move something from one place to another
transferred, transferring

translate to give the meaning in another language
translator, translation, translating

transparent clear enough to be seen through
transparency

transport to carry from one place to another

trap an instrument for catching animals
trapped, trapping, trapper, trapdoor

trapeze a circus swing high above the ground

travel to go from one place to another
travelled, travelling, traveller

trawler a fishing-boat that drags a net

tray a flat board for carrying things

treacle a dark sticky liquid made from sugar
treacly

tread 1. to put your foot on the ground
2. the pattern cut into a tyre
trod, trodden

treasure something that has great value

treasurer someone who looks after money

treat 1. to behave in a certain way towards someone (He treats his dog cruelly.)
2. something that gives unusual pleasure
treatment

tree a large plant with a trunk ▶
treeless

tremble to shiver or shake
trembling

trench a narrow ditch dug in the ground

trespass to go into someone's property without permission
trespasses, trespasser

triangle a shape with three sides
triangular

tribe a group of people belonging together and ruled by one chief
tribal, tribesmen

trick something done to cheat or mislead
trickery, tricky

trickle a slow thin flow of water
trickling

tricycle a three-wheeled cycle

trifle 1. something of very little importance
2. a pudding made of custard, cream and cake
trifling

trigger the part you pull to fire a gun

trim 1. neat and tidy

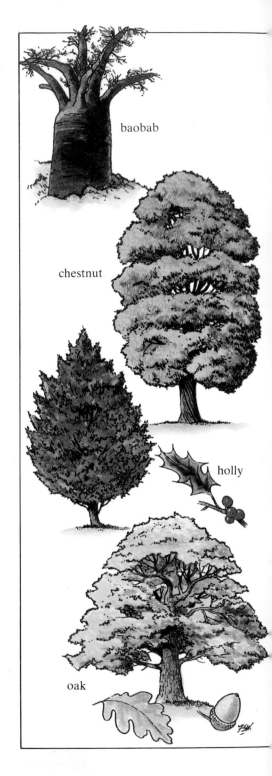

baobab

chestnut

holly

oak

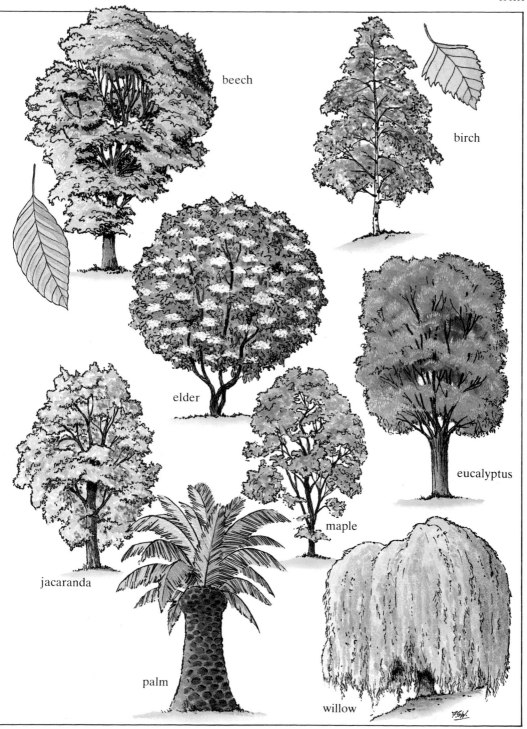

beech

birch

elder

eucalyptus

jacaranda

maple

palm

willow

145

red cedar

fir

monkey puzzle

pine

2. to cut away the unwanted edge
3. to decorate (a dress trimmed with lace)
trimmed, trimming, trimmings

trio a group of three

trip 1. to catch the foot and fall
2. a journey
tripped, tripping, tripper

triumph a victory; great success
triumphant, triumphantly

trolley 1. a small hand-cart
2. a small table on wheels
trolley-bus

tropics the hot parts of the world either side of the equator
tropical, Tropic of Cancer, Tropic of Capricorn

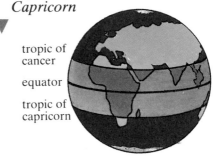

tropic of cancer

equator

tropic of capricorn

trot to move with gentle steps
trotted, trotting, trotter

trouble anything that causes worry or difficulty
troublesome, troubling

trough a narrow box for animals to feed or drink from

trousers a garment with two legs

trout a freshwater fish

trowel 1. a small hand-tool for planting (See page 141)
2. a tool for spreading cement or plaster

truant a child who stays away from school without permission
truancy

truck 1. a vehicle for carrying heavy loads; a lorry
2. an open railway wagon

true correct; faithful
truly, truth
trumpet a musical instrument (See
page 90)
trunk 1. the main stem of a tree
2. an elephant's long nose
3. a large box for carrying clothes
trust to believe in the goodness or
honesty of someone
trustful, trustworthy, trustingly
truth whatever is true
truthful, truthfully
try 1. to have a go; to attempt
2. to test (Try this for size.)
3. a score in rugby
tried, tries, trier, trying
T-shirt a close-fitting shirt
tuatara a New Zealand reptile

tulip a flower with a bulb
tumble to fall down
tumbling, tumble-down
tumbler a drinking glass

tub a round container
tubby
tube 1. a hollow length of metal, glass,
plastic, etc.
2. the underground railway line in
London
Tuesday the third day of the week
tug 1. to pull hard
2. a small powerful boat to pull
others
tugged, tugging

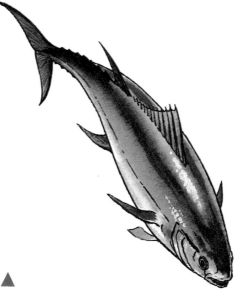

tuna a large sea-fish
tune a set of musical notes making a
pleasant sound
*tuneful, tunefully, tuning-fork,
tuneless*
tunnel an underground passage
turban a hat made by wrapping a long
piece of material round and round
your head
turf a piece of earth with grass growing
in it

▲

turkey a large farmyard bird

turn 1. to move round like a wheel
2. to move and face a different direction
3. the proper time for someone to do something (It's your turn to cook.)

turnip a root vegetable

turtle a water animal like a tortoise

▼

tusk a long pointed tooth

tweed a thick woollen cloth

tweezers a tool for gripping small things

twelve the number 12
twelfth

twenty the number 20
twenties, twentieth

twice two times

twig a small branch of a tree

twilight the dim light between sunset and darkness

twin one of two born at the same time to the same mother

twinkle to shine like stars in the sky; to glitter
twinkling

twist to turn something round

two the number 2
second

type 1. a kind
2. to print words by using a typewriter
typing, typist, typewriter

tyrant a cruel ruler
tyranny, tyrannical, tyrannize

tyre a rubber ring round a wheel

Uu

ugly not pretty; unpleasant to look at
uglier, ugliest, ugliness
ukelele a musical instrument

umbrella a covered frame to keep you dry
umpire someone who judges a game
unable not able
unaware not aware
uncertain not certain; doubtful
uncertainly, uncertainty
uncle the brother of your mother or father; the husband of your aunt
uncomfortable not comfortable
uncomfortably, uncomfortableness

uncommon not common; unusual
unconscious not conscious; not aware
under below; beneath
underclothes, underground, undercarriage, underline, underneath, underwear
understand to know the meaning of something
understandable, understood
undertake to agree to do something
undertaking, undertook, undertaker
undo to untie or unfasten
undoes, undone, undid
undress to take off your clothes
unequal not the same in size or amount
unequalled, unequally
uneven not even; not level
unexpected not expected; surprising
unfair not fair
unfaithful not faithful
ungrateful not showing thankfulness
unhappy not happy; sad
unhappily, unhappiness
unicorn an imaginary animal like a horse with a horn
uniform 1. special clothes worn by soldiers, policemen, schoolchildren, etc.
2. the same; not varying

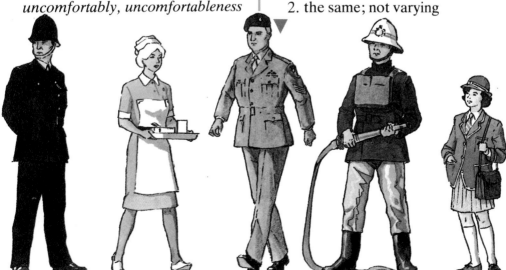

union being joined together or united
trade union
unite to join together
unity, uniting
universe everything that exists
universal, universally
university a place where students
study for degrees
universities
unkind not kind
unkindly, unkindness
unknown not known
unless if not (I shall be late unless I
hurry.)
unlike different from
unload to take a load off
unlucky out of luck
unluckily, unluckiness
unnecessary not necessary
unnecessarily
unpleasant not pleasant; nasty
unpopular not popular; disliked
unqualified not qualified
untidy not tidy
untidily, untidiness
untie to undo what has been tied
untied, unties, untying
until up to the time when
untrue not true
untruth
unusual not usual; strange
unwell ill
unwilling not willing
unwrap to take out of its wrapping
unwrapped, unwrapping
uphill up a slope
upper the higher part
upright 1. standing up straight
2. honest
uproar a great noise of shouting
upset 1. to overturn
2. to make unhappy
upsetting
upside-down turned over so that the
top is at the bottom

upstairs on the floor above
up-to-date modern
upward to a higher position
upwards
urgent needing to be done at once
urgently, urgency
use to do something with
using, usable
useful helpful; of use
usefully, usefulness
useless without any use
uselessly, uselessness
usher a person who shows you to your
seat
usual normal; often done
usually
utter 1. to speak
2. total (utter darkness)

Vv

vacant empty
vacancy, vacancies
vacation a holiday
vaccinate to inject against smallpox
vaccinating, vaccination
vacuum an empty space without air
vacuum-cleaner, vacuum-flask

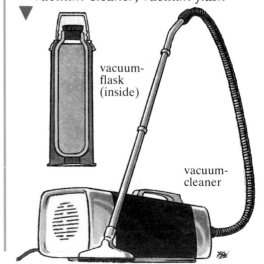

vacuum-
flask
(inside)

vacuum-
cleaner

vagabond a tramp

vague not clear; not sure
vaguely, vagueness

vain 1. conceited about your ability or looks
2. useless (a vain attempt)
vainly, vanity

valentine a card sent on 14th February, St Valentine's Day

valley low ground between two hills

value the importance or worth of something
valueless

valuable of great value

valve 1. a device for controlling the flow of gas or liquid
2. an electronic device in radio

van a covered vehicle for carrying loads

vanish to go out of sight

vanity too much pride in yourself

vapour mist or steam

various of different sorts

vary to be different; to change
varied, varies, variety, varieties

vase a jar for holding flowers

vast very large; huge

veal the meat from a calf

vegetable any plant other than fruit used for food

vegetarian a person who does not eat meat

vehicle something like a car, lorry, cart, or sledge that is used to carry people or things

veil a thin covering, especially for the face

vein one of the thin tubes that carry blood round the body

velvet a thick soft silky cloth

venison meat from a deer

veranda a roofed but open platform outside a house

verb a word that expresses action

verdict the decision reached by a jury or judge at the end of a court trial

vermin any harmful wild creature such as rats, mice, lice etc

verse a set of lines in a song or poem

vertical straight up and down

vessel 1. a container for liquids
2. a ship

vest an undergarment worn next to the skin

vet a short name for a veterinary surgeon; an animal doctor

vex to annoy or make angry

viaduct a long bridge with many arches

vibrate to move rapidly to and fro
vibrating, vibration

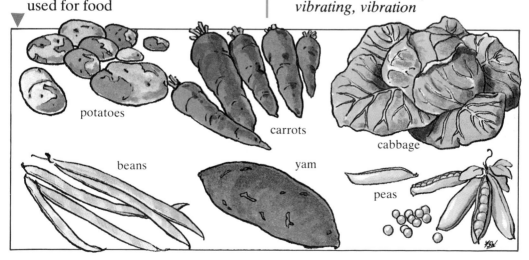

potatoes

carrots

cabbage

beans

yam

peas

vicar a clergyman who looks after a parish

vice-captain the person who may take the place of a captain when necessary

victim someone who suffers
victimize, victimization

victory the winning of a game or battle
victor, victorious, victories

video a device for recording television programmes for replaying

view something to be looked at; a scene
viewer, viewless

village a place in the country where a number of people live

villain a bad man; a wrong-doer
villainy, villainous

vine a plant on which grapes grow
vineyard

vinegar a sharp liquid to flavour food

violent being strong and causing harm
violently, violence

violet a small flower

violin a musical instrument (See page 90)

virtue any good quality such as goodness, honesty, kindness
virtuous

virus a thing too small to be seen, which can cause disease; a germ

visible able to be seen
visibly, visibility, vision

visit to go and see someone or some place
visitor

vitamin a substance needed for health and growth (Vitamin C is found in oranges.)

vivid bright and clear

vocabulary a list of words; all the words a person uses

voice the sound of speaking or singing

volcano a mountain that may erupt and throw out liquid rock and hot ashes
volcanoes, volcanic

volt a unit for measuring electric power
voltage

volume 1. a book
2. the amount of space taken up by a thing

voluntary done because you are willing to do it
voluntarily, volunteer

vomit to be sick; to throw up
vomited, vomiting

vote to choose by making a sign
voting, voter

vowel one of the letters a,e,i,o,u; any sound that is not a consonant

voyage a journey by sea

vulgar rude; ill-mannered
vulgarly, vulgarity

vulture a large bird that feeds on dead animals (See opposite page)

Ww

waddle to walk like a duck
waddling

wade to walk through water
wading, waders

wafer a very thin biscuit

wag to move quickly from side to side
wagged, wagging

wage 1. money paid weekly for work done
2. to fight (to wage war)

wagon 1. an open railway truck
2. a four-wheeled cart pulled by horses

waist the part of your body between your chest and hips
waistcoat, waist-high, waistline

wait 1. to stay in one place till something happens
2. to serve food at table
waiter, waitress, waiting-room

wake 1. to stop sleeping
2. the track left in the water by a boat
waking, woke, woken

walk to move on your feet
walking-stick, walk-over

walkie-talkie a radio telephone that can be carried around

wall a side of a house or a fence made of bricks or stone
wallpaper, wallflower

wallaby a small kind of kangaroo
wallabies

wallet a pocket case for money and papers

walrus a sea animal with tusks
walruses

wander to move about aimlessly
want to need or wish for something
war a fight between countries
warfare, warcry, war-head, warlike, warring, warship

man-of-war

dreadnought battleship

destroyer

warder someone who looks after prisoners
wardrobe a cupboard for clothes
warm 1. fairly hot
2. to heat (Warm your hands by the fire.)
warmth, warmly

warn to tell someone about difficulties or trouble before they happen
warrior a fighting man, a soldier
wash to make clean with water
washable, washes, washing-machine

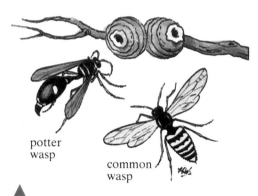

potter wasp

common wasp

wasp a stinging insect
waste 1. to use up carelessly
2. rubbish; anything not wanted
wasteful, wastefully, wasting, waster
watch 1. to look at for some time
2. a time-keeper for the wrist
3. to be on guard
watches, watchful, watchfully, watcher, watchman
water the colourless liquid found in rivers and seas
water-closet, water-colour, watercress, waterfall, watering-can, water-lily, waterlogged, water-polo, waterproof, watertight, waterworks, watery
watt a unit of electrical power
wave 1. a moving line of water that breaks on the shore
2. to move from side to side (You wave your hand to say good-bye.)
waving, waver
wax a substance that melts and is used to make candles and polish
way 1. how something is done
2. a path, road or direction
wayside, waylay, waylaid

weak not strong
weaken, weakness
wealth a lot of money or property
wealthy, wealthier, wealthiest
weapon anything used for fighting
wear 1. to have clothes on your body
2. to show signs of too much use
weary tired
wearily, weariness
weather how wet or hot the air is
outside
weave to make threads into cloth
weaver, weaving
web the net spun by a spider
web-footed
wedding a marriage ceremony
*wed, wedded, wedding-ring,
wedding-cake*
wedge a V-shaped object for fixing
things
Wednesday the fourth day of the week
weed a wild plant growing where it is
not wanted
weedy, weediness

week a period of seven days
week-day, week-end, weekly
weep to cry; to shed tears
wept
weigh to measure how heavy
something is
*weighing-machine, weight,
weightless, weighty*
weird very strange
welcome to show you are pleased when
someone arrives
welcoming
well 1. in good health
2. in a good way
3. a deep hole to reach water or oil
well-being
wellingtons long rubber boots
west one of the points of the compass
westerly, western, westward
wet not dry; covered with water
*wetness, wetted, wetter, wettest,
wetting*
whale a sea animal like a large fish
whaler, whaling

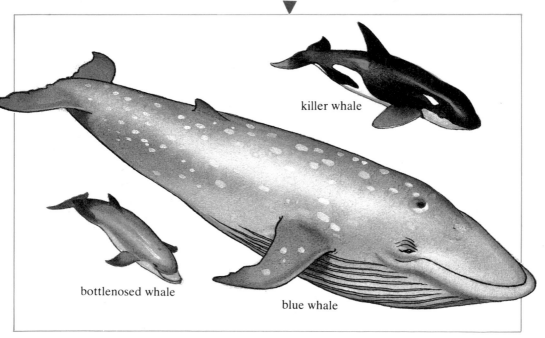

killer whale

bottlenosed whale

blue whale

wharf a platform where ships are loaded or unloaded
wharfs

wheat a cereal used for flour (See page 29)

wheel an object that turns on an axle
wheelbarrow, wheel-chair

whether if (I don't know whether this is the right address.)

while 1. during the time that (You wait here while I find out.)
2. a period of time (I waited a long while.)

whimper to cry softly

whine to give long sad sounds
whining

whinny to make a sound like a horse

whip 1. a piece of string or leather on a handle
2. to beat with a whip; to beat cream till stiff
whipped, whipping, whipper

whirl to move round and round very rapidly
whirlpool, whirlwind

whiskers hair growing on the face

whisky a strong alcoholic drink

whisper to speak very softly

whistle 1. to make high sound by blowing through your lips
2. an instrument that makes a whistling sound
whistler, whistling

white the colour of clean snow
whiten, whiter, whitest

whole complete; in one piece
wholly, wholemeal, wholesale

wick the strip of material that burns in candles and oil-lamps

wicked very bad; evil

wicket 1. the three stumps and bails in cricket
2. the strip of ground between the two wickets
wicket-keeper

wide 1. broad
2. measured from side to side (The table is 1 metre wide.)
widen, widely, widespread, width

widow a woman whose husband has died

widower a man whose wife has died

wife a married woman
wives

wig false hair covering the head

wigwam a tent or hut lived in by American Indians

wild 1. living freely; not tamed
2. fierce; stormy

wildebeest the gnu, a South African antelope

wilderness a stretch of wild country where no-one lives

wilful too strong-willed; obstinate
wilfully, wilfulness

willing ready to do something
willingly, willingness

willow a tree with thin branches (See page 145)

win to beat your rivals
winner, winning, won

wind − rhyming with 'sinned' − a steady movement of air
windless, windy, windiness, windmill, windscreen, wind-cheater, wind instruments

windmill

wind − rhyming with 'mind' − 1. to
turn and twist (a winding road)
2. to tighten by coiling
wound

window an opening in the wall of a
house to let in light
*window-box, window-frame,
window-pane, window-sill*

wine a strong drink made from grapes

wing the part of a bird, insect or
aeroplane that keeps it up when
flying

wink to close and open one eye quickly

winter the season between autumn
and spring
wintry

wipe to dry or clean by rubbing with a
cloth
wiping, wipers

wire long thin pieces of metal
wiring, wireless

wise understanding; sensible
wisely, wisdom

wish a desire; a longing
wishes, wish-bone, wishful thinking

wit clever amusing talk
witty, wittier, wittiest, wittily

witch a woman supposed to be able to
make magic
witches, witchcraft

within inside

witness someone who sees something
happen
witnesses

wizard a man supposed to have
magical powers

wobble to move unsteadily from side
to side
wobbling, wobbly, wobbliness

wolf a wild animal like a large dog
wolves

▼

woman a female person; a lady
women

wonder 1. a feeling of surprise
2. to ask oneself
wonderful, wonderfully

wood 1. the hard part of a tree
2. a place where many trees grow
*wooded, wooden, woodland,
woodwork*

woodpecker a bird

▼

157

wool the hair from sheep
woollen, woolly
word one of the units that make up language
wordy, wordiness, wordless
work what you have to do to earn a living; a job
workable, workbench, worker, workmen, workshop, workmanship
world the earth and everything on it
worldly, worldliness, world-wide
worm a long thin wriggling creature that lives in the ground or water

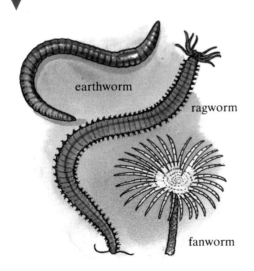

earthworm
ragworm
fanworm

worry to feel troubled; to be uneasy
worries, worried, worrier, worrying
worship to admire and love
worshipped, worshipping, worshipper
worth having a certain value
worthless, worthy, worthwhile
wound an injury to the body
wrap to cover something all round
wrapped, wrapper, wrapping
wreath a circle of flowers or leaves
wreck 1. to ruin or destroy
2. a ruin, especially a ship
wrecker, wreckage

wren a small bird
wrestle to struggle with a person
wrestler, wrestling
wriggle to make quick twisting movements
wriggling, wriggler
wrinkle a small crease or line
wrinkling, wrinkled
wrist the joint between your arm and your hand
write to make letters and words on paper
writing, written, wrote
wrong 1. not correct
2. not right or good (It is wrong to steal.)
wrongful, wrong-doer, wrong-doing

Xx

Xmas a way of writing Christmas
X-ray to photograph the inside of someone
X-rays, X-rayed
xylophone a musical instrument

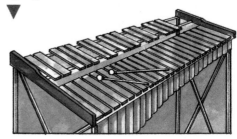

Yy

yacht a sailing boat
yachtsman
yak a long-haired ox from Asia

yard 1. a measure of length; about 91 centimetres
2. an open space surrounded by walls
yarn 1. a story
2. thread
yawn to open your mouth wide and breathe in deeply when tired
year 12 months
yearly
yell to shout or scream loudly
yellow the colour of a ripe lemon
yesterday the day before today
yew an evergreen tree

yield 1. to give in; to surrender
2. the amount produced (a good yield of wheat)
yogurt a food made from sour milk
yolk the yellow part of an egg
young not grown up; not old
youngster
youth 1. the early part of a person's life
2. a young person
youthful
yo-yo a toy that moves up and down on a string

Zz

zeal great enthusiasm
zealous
zebra a wild animal like a horse with black and white stripes
zebra crossing

zero nought; the figure 0
zigzag a line with many sharp turns
zigzagged, zigzagging
zip a fastener with small teeth that come together
zipped, zipper
zone an area
zoo a place to go to see specially kept wild animals
zoom to fly suddenly upwards

Things to Do

There are lots of things to do with this dictionary. You can look up words you do not understand or cannot spell, you can see what certain objects and animals look like – and you can have plenty of fun.

See how one word leads to another. From *bed,* we get *bedroom* and *bedtime,* from *fright,* we get *frighten, frightful* and *frightfully.* Choose words yourself and see how many related words you can think of.

Some words have more than one meaning: *box, code, cone* are examples. See how many more you can think of or find in the dictionary.

An anagram is a word made from the letters of another word. For example, the letters of *live* can also spell *evil.* Can you make these anagrams?

1. Make *end* into a place where lions live.
2. Make *reed* into a very fast animal.
3. Make *cheap* into a fruit.
4. Make *shore* into an animal you ride.
5. Make *felt* into the opposite of *right.*
6. Make *rats* into a heavenly body.
7. Make *palm* into something that gives light.
8. Change *bleat* into a piece of furniture.
9. Change *skid* into young goats.
10. Change *plate* into a part of a flower.

Can you make the new words by changing only one letter in the word? The first one is *dove.*

1.	done	a bird
2.	horse	a dwelling
3.	care	a mammal
4.	mill	a drink
5.	chain	a seat
6.	bed	an insect
7.	spark	a fish
8.	lamb	a light
9.	fast	a direction
10.	cats	a cereal

Here is an example beginning with c of each item in the list. Can you find an example beginning with l of each?

1.	a bird	canary
2.	a mammal	camel
3.	a fish	cod
4.	a shellfish	crab
5.	a fruit	cherry
6.	a vegetable	carrot
7.	a tree	cedar
8.	a drink	cocoa
9.	a boat	cruiser
10.	a vehicle	car

In a word ladder, to change the top word into the bottom one, you have to change one letter at a time and make a new word each time, like this:

ten
tin
sin
six

Can you change *cat* into *dog* in the same way? When you have done so, try *wood* into *coal.*